In 2012 Julie Randall was diagnosed with stage four metastatic advanced melanoma and given only months to live. She believes that sharing her incredible story of survival against the odds may help others who are undergoing a similar journey and spread hope to those who need it. Julie has written for and spoken at conferences and fundraisers for Bristol-Myers Squibb pharmaceuticals and the Providence Cancer Center in Oregon, USA. Julie lives on the Northern Beaches of Sydney and is married with two daughters. *Patient 71* is her first book.

PATIENT 71

PATIENT 71

JULIE RANDALL

woodhall press

woodhall press

Woodhall Press, 81 Old Saugatuck Road, Norwalk, CT 06855
WoodhallPress.com

Library of Congress Cataloging-in-Publication Data available
ISBN 978-1-949116-97-7 (paper: alk paper)
ISBN 978-1-949116-98-4 (electronic)
First Edition
Distributed by Independent Publishers Group
(800) 888-4741
Printed in the United States of America

For Scott.

Your unequivocal love and belief helped me live to honour
my promise to our daughters.
I love being your wife.

Author's Note

This is a story about a woman, me, who thought her life was just about perfect. I had a husband I adored and two precious daughters, an amazing family and friends and a great job. Who could ask for more?

I had just turned 50 and was grappling with that number. I'd soon come to learn it was actually a privilege. I was healthy and happy.

I'd lost my mum too early to cancer and held my sister's hand as she suffered through the same disease. Then, shortly after my birthday celebrations, my world spun out of control. I was told I was going to die and given a brochure on palliative care.

Even though I hid the worst of my diagnosis from my girls, seeing their despair started a fire that raged inside of me. I couldn't accept my fate. So I made a promise to my daughters.

I promised them I would live. I stood on the edge of the abyss but refused to fall in. I wasn't ready. Are any of us?

I searched the globe for answers and found a possible lifeline, a miracle it seemed.

This book is about how I clawed my way back and what I discovered along the way. Strap yourself in, it's a bumpy ride . . .

Chapter One

It was Thursday 21 June 2012, the traffic was humming along nicely and I was on top of the world. It was the last day of my working week and, to make things even sweeter, my work friend Delfina and I were being taken out for lunch by one of the directors, which would hopefully include a couple of cheeky sauvignon blancs and no doubt a few laughs.

Life was good. I had just celebrated my 50th birthday the previous Saturday night with a rocking party that went till the wee hours. I called it my 'Forty Tenth' on the invitations, demonstrating a strong passion to hang on to my forties and basically just being a smart arse.

It would soon become crystal clear to me that every birthday is a gift and being unhappy about the number, whatever it may be, is sacrilege.

Yes, it was one of those days when you drive along singing loudly, and badly, with the radio blaring, appreciating everyone and everything. I was thanking the universe for my wonderful life, my mostly beautiful husband, my girls, my sisters, brother, dad, friends, the sun, the trees, you name it, I was appreciating it.

'You ladies ready?' asked Pete the director later that morning, as Delfina and I touched up our lippie and put on our jackets.

Yep we were ready. It felt like I'd just sat down at my desk and we were already off for a long lazy lunch. *Could this day get any better?*

Del and I had been a little excited as it wasn't every day, actually *never*, that a director took the office staff out to lunch. Pete said he wanted to show his appreciation for our hard work and we didn't argue. I had worked for a marine rescue organisation in Sydney's CBD for six years and this definitely was not a common occurrence.

We went down in the lift and out into the sunshine; it was a little chilly, but who cared? We were going to the Opera Bar on the foreshores of Sydney Harbour, then to an upmarket Chinese restaurant overlooking the water with an uninterrupted view of the Harbour Bridge, Luna Park and the Opera House. It was picture perfect. I will never tire of that vista.

We dined on duck curry, chilli scallops and a very spicy beef dish. I talked Delfina into a glass of wine; she didn't drink much, and I remember she was giggling a lot. Pete was telling us some great stories from his days in the navy; he liked to do that and we liked to listen.

Well, like all good times, it was over much too soon and we made our way (as slowly as possible) back to the office, taking in all the sights along the way. I definitely would have gone even more slowly, backwards perhaps, if I'd known what was up ahead.

We said goodbye to Pete, who was making his way back home to Port Stephens north of Sydney, then Delfina and I made our way up to the fifth floor in the lift.

As I walked to my desk and sat down, my friend Frans asked me what I had for lunch. I couldn't answer him. It was strange. Something wasn't right. I took a few steps towards the bathroom and stopped, then turned to him and said, 'I feel weird, I can't find my words'.

He looked at me and motioned for me to sit on a chair in the foyer. 'I'll keep an eye on you,' he said in a calm but concerned voice.

I don't know how much time passed; it could have been ten minutes, it could have been two hours. The next thing I remember was my name being shouted over and over again, 'Julie, Julie, Julie!' I could hear it but I couldn't respond.

Finally I opened my eyes. My head was hanging down. It was another one of my colleagues, Heinz, calling my name. He was flanked by two paramedics, a male and a female, who were hooking me up to devices, asking me my name and if I knew what day it was.

The rest of my co-workers were in the background with looks of horror on their faces. Holy shit! What the fuck was going on? The nausea was intense. I cannot remember ever feeling so sick in my life. It turns out I'd just had a massive brain seizure right there in the office.

The paramedics put me on a trolley, we went down from the fifth floor, my workmate Kate was with me and that was the end of my career at Marine Rescue New South Wales.

Just like that, it was over.

'I'm never eating Chinese food again,' I said as they wheeled me away, always trying to make light of a bad situation. But somehow I knew I was in trouble.

I was taken to St Vincent's Hospital Emergency Room; it was manic, bright lights, face masks, people rushing everywhere. Before I knew it my daughter Morgan and her boyfriend rushed in, closely followed by my husband, Scott. I can only imagine what receiving that phone call would have been like; it is still raw for all of us and always will be.

Scott tried to reassure me that this was probably just a one-off episode. 'We've been celebrating your 50th birthday for the last week, you're just tired that's all.'

I hoped he was right, I really did, but perception and instinct can be powerful. I knew this was serious with every fibre of my being.

The next move was to scan my brain. Now you would think an MRI would be the least of my worries under the circumstances, but it wasn't. I am extremely claustrophobic and had at least three false starts, pressing the buzzer and calling out for the radiographer to get me the hell out of there, before Scott finally came in, held my feet and yelled to me over the top of the clanging noise of the machine.

'It's okay, I'm here, it will be over soon.' Then, 'Not long to go now,' he said reassuringly, 'nearly finished.'

For fifteen minutes he did all he could to comfort me, but I knew he was doing his very best to keep it together as well.

The tears were streaming down my face inside the MRI machine, but I couldn't wipe them, I wasn't allowed to move. I just had to let them flow. Inside my head I was screaming out, *Please, please, please make this stop!*

Next, as we were soon to learn would be a painful constant, we had to wait. I guess an hour had gone by when a lovely doctor with a crooked nose walked into the room and without hesitation proclaimed, 'You have a brain tumour in your left blah blah blah and blah blah blah.'

Well that's what it sounded like to me because my head started spinning and I went into shock.

Scott later told me the doctor said, 'Don't panic yet, it could be benign and you've just had a bleed causing the seizure. It's in a pretty good spot in terms of removal.'

While Scott seemed positive and happy about this news, I wasn't feeling his joy. I'm a very positive person, but in that moment I had a powerful sense that this wasn't good at all.

A CT scan was next to check the rest of my body. Not so bad this time as it didn't involve being trapped inside a horrible, noisy machine.

I spent most of the night in the Emergency Room, which is infamous for battling with drug addicts and criminals, and that Thursday night did not let the ER's reputation down.

Outside my cubicle was a guy, an ice addict, restrained and strapped to his bed in a straitjacket, who was yelling obscenities at the nurses while continually trying to untie himself.

I wanted to yell out, *Shut the fuck up!*

But I was afraid he would succeed with his escape and come in and attack me. I could see him through the curtain; he looked scary.

Oh my god, this is a nightmare, this can't be real, I kept saying to myself. *This morning I was the happiest girl in the world. Now I am lonely and terrified.*

I'd sent Scott home to be with our daughters, Morgan and Remy. They needed him and so did I, but he couldn't be in two places at once.

Finally a tall male nurse with a green hospital coat came and moved me to another bed so that I could 'get some sleep'. Yeah right!

I was transferred to a large room with three elderly people who were moaning and groaning and making noises I'd never heard before.

I watched re-runs of *Flipper* and *Gilligan's Island* on the small TV Scott had organised for me. But ten seconds didn't go by without my mind coming back to my reality. *I have a brain tumour, a BRAIN TUMOUR.* Was I really saying that?

At best it was a benign tumour that would still require brain surgery.

'Yes, Julie, brain surgery, there's no other way,' the doctor had said.

At worst it was a malignant tumour which meant I had cancer and would require surgery and who knew what else?

You don't have to be Stephen Hawking to know that brain cancer does not usually have a happy ending.

That was the longest night of my life.

Chapter Two

I'll take you back to the beginning. I arrived in the world at 2.20pm on 8 June 1962 at St Margaret's Hospital in Sydney with a head full of unusually white hair. I was a little sister to my brother Mark and my sister Kerri and would end up being the middle child when my sisters Michelle and Nicole were born. We did have an older brother, Mum's firstborn. His name was Wayne but tragically he died at 39 weeks in her womb. Dad says Mum never got over losing Wayne. She had to give birth to him and then the hospital staff took him away. She didn't get to say hello *or* goodbye.

I can only imagine the utter grief, emptiness and sense of loss Mum and Dad felt that day, an ache in their hearts that could never be filled. Mum didn't talk about Wayne much when we were growing up; when she did she would put her head down and stare at the floor. It must have been too painful for her to make eye contact. Thinking about it now makes my own heart ache.

For the early years of our lives we lived out the back of an old haberdashery store in Kensington with Mum's parents. My grandfather died of emphysema when I was two and we then moved north to Warriewood Beach with Nanna Sharkey in tow. Mum and Dad had bought a block of land in their pursuit of the great Australian dream and built what was to become our beloved brick and timber five-bedroom family home. We were also lucky to have Dad's parents, Nanny and Pa, living down the street.

When my youngest sister, Nicole, came along in 1969 there were eight of us in that brick and timber house. It was a crazy, busy, fun household with lots of laughs, lots of fun and lots of fights. You had to learn very quickly how to stick up for yourself *and* how to get noticed.

While my sisters were playing with dolls I would be making up little pantomimes in my head. I would create characters and have full conversations with them. Sometimes out loud. It was my own world that I could escape to, a place that no one else could enter. Sometimes I would bring the characters to life and pretend they had infiltrated my body to scare my two younger sisters. Pretty weird *and* mean now I think about it. One of my characters was called 'Cathy Ghost Head'. You'd think I could have come up with something a little more creative than that. I would say to my sisters. 'I'm not Julie . . . I'm Cathy Ghost Head.'

And they would freak out and ask, 'Where's Julie?' and then I would snap back to Julie and they would say, 'Cathy was here!' I'd pretend I didn't know what they were talking about. How cruel was that? They still tell me I have a lot to answer for.

Being the middle child I sometimes felt neither here nor there so by the time I turned seven I had devised a plan to attract my mother's full attention. I would get really good at netball, the sport she lived and breathed. Coaching netball teams was her passion in life. So I spent every afternoon in the backyard shooting goals into a ring my dad had erected. I wouldn't go inside until I had successfully shot a hundred. I would also invite school friends around and make them throw me the ball so I could perfect my catching and passing. Then I literally counted down the days until I could trial for the Manly-Warringah under ten representative netball team. I made the team and played rep netball until I was twenty when my passion for touch football took over.

Being in the rep team, I gained my mother's full attention but not always in the way I wanted it. Mum was the coach of a few of those teams and would be harder on me than anyone else. If I spoke out of line I was put on the bench. '"Left right out" is your position now,' she would whisper in my ear.

Mum was tough. Hilariously funny, but tough. 'Wake up to yourself' was a common phrase in our house and whingeing wasn't tolerated. If you were in trouble at school you deserved it. If you didn't want to train for a sport, she wouldn't let you play. If you wanted to achieve something you worked your bum off for it. We were brought up to be tough and not to take shit from anyone. She taught us that we were not above or below others.

If you complained about your job Mum would say, 'Nobody likes their job.' Mum called a spade a spade. There weren't many verbal expressions of love, but actions spoke louder than words. She would have taken a bullet for us without hesitation and we all knew that for sure.

Dad is funny too. When we were kids he tried to be tough but his soft, loving nature prevailed. He used to spoil us rotten, much to Mum's disgust. Dad did teach us respect, though. When he got cranky you found somewhere to hide. You could only push him so far.

Life was good. We were sports-crazy and always on the go. Laziness was not an option. The theory was that being busy kept you out of trouble and for the most part it worked. On the weekends we would go to church and parties at Mum and Dad's friends' houses, where we would have a blast. We would dance and sing to Neil Diamond and Mum taught us how to rock'n'roll.

When Mum and Dad went to work, Nanna Sharkey looked after us. She was our family's Alice from *The Brady Bunch*. Mum and Dad would rise at 6am and head to work in the city. Nanna would make us breakfast then get the five of us off to school, do the housework and have warm scones and jam on the table when we came home. Then she would oversee our homework while cooking the evening meal. Mum and Dad would arrive home at around 5.30 and the eight of us would sit around the table laughing and fighting and teasing each other. They were the best of times.

I left school after graduating from Stella Maris College in Manly in Year Ten. One morning not too long afterwards, I was woken up by the Positions Vacant section of the newspaper being placed over my head. I duly got a job in a bank, which I hated, but since Mum had always said nobody liked their job, I persevered for about five years. After I left the bank, I joined an advertising firm and stayed for twenty years. I absolutely loved that job.

The fun theme continued well into my twenties with lots of boys, partying and travel. Then on an unusually warm Sunday afternoon in August 1987, after cheering on a local football team, my girlfriends Kara and Lorica and I decided to call in to a local pub and there he was. 'He's mine,' I announced as I locked eyes with a blond-haired, blue-eyed, tanned hunk of spunk. I bought him a drink, wedged him into a corner and sat next to him so he couldn't escape. Then I fed him a few more drinks and convinced him I was the girl of his dreams. His name was Scott Randall. He became my husband and the love of my life. Thank goodness he didn't know what he was in for when he signed that marriage certificate in 1991 because if he did and had one ounce of common sense, he would have run for the hills as fast as he could.

Scott and I welcomed our daughter Morgan in 1992 and then Remy in 1995. Scott loved the idea of having girls as he'd grown up in a house full of boys. We were blissfully happy with our own gorgeous little family on the Northern Beaches.

Sometimes it felt like our family had had such a beautiful life growing up, too beautiful because for whatever reason the pendulum had begun to swing. It felt like the universe had decided it had been too good for too long. Things changed forever when my mother was taken from us so young.

One night in November 1998 my mother called, crying while breaking the news that she had lung cancer. I was completely gutted. Then if that wasn't devastating enough, my sister Michelle was diagnosed with breast cancer three weeks later. I can't begin to tell you how utterly shattered that news left me and it was at this time that our family came to the soul-destroying realisation that our beautiful life, the life with which we had been blessed for four decades, was over. The following months passed in a blur, and we all did our best to support our loved ones, and each other. Somehow we managed to bear the unbearable. Michelle recovered.

A decade passed as we tried to put our lives back together. Then everything fell apart again. It was my turn.

Chapter Three

The sun came up as it does and beamed through the hospital windows. It was now light, but my world had become dark. On the surface it was another beautiful Sydney winter's day but in total contrast to the day before I was now asking the universe what the hell was going on.

Why was I here in this god-forsaken place with three very old sick people as my roommates? Why, after all the thanking and appreciating I did the day before, was I now here, scared senseless about my future? The questions just kept running over and over in my head.

I wanted to see my husband, my Rock of Gibraltar. It was torture not having him with me on that long excruciating night. The temptation to call him was intense but I was hoping he was getting some sleep. It turns out we were both thinking the same thing. Stupid, really. How could either of us expect the other to be sleeping?

At about 9am, Scott walked through the door. He gave me an awkward little smile and I tried to smile back but instead I burst into tears.

He sat down next to me and held me tightly, like he was never going to let me go and when I looked up at him the tears were streaming down his face. He was still trying to comfort me, telling me that this might all be okay, but I could tell he was scared. I could see the fear in his eyes.

'How are the girls?' I asked.

'Worried,' he replied softly. But it cut like a knife.

I didn't want them to be worried about me. They were teenagers, I wanted them to be swanning around, not a care in the world, their biggest concern being what they would wear out that night. I love our girls so much and just like all parents I would take a bullet for them. I just couldn't stand the thought of them worrying about me.

Scott and I tried hard to talk about other things like work, the weather, the skiing trip to Japan we had booked three weeks earlier. We talked as if we were still going, but I knew we weren't. He was trying to distract me with magazines, cups of tea and offerings of food, but the distraction didn't last long and we kept going back to the same questions over and over again.

Where's the doctor? What's going on? Where are the results from the CT scan? Was this a benign growth that could easily be removed or was it something more? Would someone please put us out of our misery?

Waiting, waiting, waiting. The entire day had gone by with no sign of a doctor. We hounded the nurses, asking them what was going on, but they just gave us one excuse after another. Finally, around 5pm, in strolled the doctor, a stocky little man with a buzz cut, flanked by three interns. They all stood in a straight line at the foot of my bed.

I didn't like him. In fact, I hated him right away just by the look on his face.

'I have the results of your CT scan,' he said.

There was a silence that seemed to go on forever.

'You have tumours in your brain, liver, lungs, pancreas and lymph nodes. Basically you have advanced cancer; it's not good news.'

No shit, I refrained from saying out loud.

I was stunned, shocked, in disbelief.

'That can't be right,' I said. 'I had a CT scan four months ago because I had some abdominal pain and there was nothing there. Nothing showed up in those organs except a couple of small cysts . . . it just can't be right.'

'Well, I'm sorry but there is now,' he said.

I put my head down and tried to tell myself this was just a bad dream and I would wake up any second. I couldn't breathe, my head was spinning, the room was spinning. Scott must have had the same response because the next thing I knew the doctor was speaking directly to him. 'You're not saying much,' he said.

'What the fuck do you want me to say?' Scott responded.

I remember thinking that was funny even under the circumstances.

The doctor went on to say he didn't know what type of cancer it was and I would have to have further tests, biopsies etc, to find out.

Fantastic, I thought, *I can't wait for that!*

From that point on, sarcasm and I became very good friends.

The doctor said I could go home, but I needed to take some medication with me to lessen the risk of having another seizure. He said it would take a while to prepare for, then continued with the fact that I would have to have the brain tumour removed sooner rather than later.

Scott and I couldn't stay in that place for one more minute, so we asked for the prescription, snatched it out of his hand and headed for the door. I didn't say goodbye to my roommates, but I don't think they knew I was there in the first place. Scott walked straight to the lift and I followed him. It felt surreal; I could have been anywhere; I wasn't in my skin, I think I still had the hospital gown on and was trailing behind him aimlessly like a scene from *One Flew Over the Cuckoo's Nest*.

We made it to the car without completely losing it, but once we were inside the floodgates opened.

'This can't be real,' I murmured over and over again. But it was. It was very real and we now had to go home and tell our two beautiful blonde-haired, blue-eyed daughters that their mum has cancer. The words that no mother ever wants to say and no child ever wants to hear.

Scott started the car and we drove away. It was Friday night and there were people everywhere in the city, laughing, drinking and having fun celebrating the end of their working week, not a care in the world.

Inconsiderate bastards, I thought, *don't they have a heart? How could they just carry on like nothing's changed? Don't they know what has just happened to us?* But as we all know, life goes on just like before, and that was a bitter pill for me to swallow.

We drove across the Harbour Bridge, which was lit up like a Christmas tree, but it had lost its appeal compared with the day before when I had been admiring its beauty over lunch.

My head was foggy; I didn't know whether to shut my eyes or keep them open. There were young people in cars everywhere with the music blaring, playing their favourite songs on their way to bars and parties. I wanted to be one of them. I had a flashback of being in my twenties driving along with my girlfriends in my blue Volkswagen singing at the tops of our voices, living in the moment, loving life. I desperately wanted to be back there.

Scott was driving in silence. I looked at him. His world had just fallen apart, it was written all over his face. He was devastated.

Our two girls were growing up fast. Morgan was nineteen and Remy sixteen. Sporty and active, they were great dancers, great touch footballers and our life had been very hectic, in a good way. They were becoming independent and we were excited about the next stage of our lives. Scott and I had been making plans to travel overseas and we were looking forward to hanging out together again like the old days, when we first started dating.

Now we were facing an uncertain, terrifying future. All our hopes and dreams had just been ripped away from us. Instead of the overseas travel, we would be travelling to cancer treatments, doctors' appointments, scans and blood tests. There would be sickness and hair loss and much more. I knew what I was in for because both my mother and my sister had been through it and it was horrible, bloody horrible, and that's putting it mildly. My sister had battled breast cancer twice, she's a survivor; but sadly I lost my mother, Beryl, when I was 39 and I still wasn't over it, I never will be. How I wanted her here on earth so badly in that moment.

I also knew what it was like to witness, to stand back and look at your loved one suffering so much and there's nothing you can do about it; you can be there, but you can't get in their head and stop the pain and that was the hardest, most heartbreaking thing I had ever gone through. How could I subject my family to that again? The thought was unbearable.

We arrived home but the house didn't look or feel the same. It even smelled different. Our adorable golden retriever, Roxy, came running over, happy as ever to see me, with her tail wagging madly. She was my shadow and would have been missing me while I was in the hospital. I didn't know what to do with myself so I went straight to the bedroom; Roxy followed.

Feeling the effects of the drugs and quite dizzy, I climbed into bed and just stared through the window into the night. I heard Morgan's footsteps coming up the stairs. I could tell everyone apart in the family just from their footsteps, so I knew who it was, and for the first time in my life I wasn't looking forward to seeing her. She came into the room, looked at me and her expression changed to horror. She knew by the way I looked back at her that I had bad news.

'I am so, so sorry to have to tell you this, Morgan. I have cancer.' I left out the advanced part.

With that she started wailing, 'No Mum! No Mum! No Mum!' She kept saying it over and over again.

She had taken the death of her grandmother very hard and the 'C' word only represented one thing to her. I kept apologising, saying that I had let her down, I had let everyone down, and I felt like a failure. I hugged her as tightly as I could and said, 'I will do everything I can, Morgan, I will fix this, I promise.'

But how would I do that? I didn't have a clue, but in that moment I had to do something to ease her pain. She was completely devastated. Then more footsteps, and I knew it was Remy. She came in and I had to break it to her as well.

'I'm so sorry, Remy. I have cancer.' I had to say those heart-wrenching words again.

She wasn't so demonstrative; she's quieter by nature. She just hugged me tightly and I could feel her shaking.

'I will fix this, I promise,' I whispered into her ear and then she left the room.

I knew she would be going somewhere to bawl her eyes out. What a nightmare.

I swallowed some sleeping pills but I still couldn't sleep; I lay awake wondering how my baby girls would cope without me. Yes they were nineteen and sixteen but as every mother knows, their children will always be their babies. I would somehow teach them to be strong; I wanted them to live a great life. They had to.

A deluge of anxiety flooded through me. The idea of ruining their lives was tearing me apart . . . they were lucky to have a wonderful father and that was comforting. Scott and the girls are extremely close; he spoils them rotten and is their tower of strength just like he is mine. But I am their mother and they needed me; I want to be there to help them navigate their lives, to cry on my shoulder when they have their hearts broken, to talk through their boy issues, to talk about their hopes and dreams, to mollycoddle them when they're sick. I want to be at their weddings, I want to be a grandmother.

By then I was a complete blubbering mess. All I could see were the things I was going to miss out on: my family, my girls, my friends, my husband, my life. I kept asking myself, *What sort of sonofabitch would take that away from us?*

My sisters would mother them, I knew that for sure. I also knew my brother and dad would rally around, I'd make sure of it. They'd be there for the girls and Scott, but I, their mother and his wife, would not and *that* was just too much to bear.

The following morning I remember hearing the awful sound of my mother-in-law crying uncontrollably and gasping for breath. She was down in the kitchen with Scott who had obviously called and told her the news.

'I can hear you,' I yelled out from the bedroom.

She was behaving like I was already dead. It was soul destroying.

Is this what I have to face? I started thinking I might as well just take the whole bottle of sleeping pills and end it now, but I couldn't; I had *promised* my children I would fix it.

How the hell was I going to do that? I had to find a way.

My family rallied around that afternoon, every single one of them, and thankfully the steroids I was taking to prevent the seizures were like uppers and had finally kicked in; they took the edge off the absolute deep despair I had been feeling. I felt like handing them out to my whole family but of course I couldn't. My father, like everyone, was heartbroken; he is the most beautiful man and this was to be the fourth time he would be witnessing one of his loved ones endure this horrific ordeal.

He is the most selfless man I have ever known and had spent the past eleven years since Mum died doing whatever he could for us kids and his grandchildren. You can count on him for anything and I knew he would be there for Scott and our girls.

The whole family sat on my bed that day. They are my best friends and confidants. We have been through so much together and I was mortified to have to put them through such torment again. But they didn't have looks of pity on their faces: they knew better, and I was grateful for that. I hate pity and I hate pity faces. Strong words, I know, but that is just who I am.

Somehow that afternoon we managed to have a beer and a laugh, believe it or not. We chatted about touch football; we are all representative players and everyone talked as if I would be playing in the upcoming state tournament we'd been training for. But I didn't share their optimism.

'Brain surgery is the next big thing in *my* calendar,' I announced. We all had a chuckle. That's the way my family rolls – we tend to laugh about things that are not laughing matters. I was so glad to have them around me. We stick together in the good times and the bad and we can always find some humour in everything, and I can tell you I needed my sense of humour like never before.

Since it was the weekend, we hadn't been able to organise any appointments. I was feeling frustrated and just wanted to find out what this thing was and how we were going to deal with it.

If I could get two peaceful minutes without thinking about having cancer I was happy, but it was never that long.

Morgan and Remy went out that Saturday night with their boyfriends. I was pleased about that; I didn't want them hanging around me being miserable and I hoped they could forget about me for just a few hours, but I was fooling myself. I later found out they cried all night long.

My poor baby girls will have that time indelibly stamped in their minds and I wish I could take it all away, but I can't, it's there forever.

Chapter Four

Monday finally came and it was time to arrange all the horrible but necessary appointments. I'd been able to get some sleep with the help of pills, and the steroids were keeping me afloat, but a deep sense of gloom gnawed at my stomach. I wished fruitlessly that I was making appointments for a massage or a facial or a manicure and pedicure – a day filled with pampering – but instead it was for GPs, oncologists, brain surgeons and pathologists. My week felt doomed.

Scott ran his own point-of-sale display business and had spent the whole of Sunday setting up his office at home so he could look after me and ferry me from one appointment to another. It was a good thing we had that flexibility because I needed him all the time. I didn't want him out of my sight. Needy? Yep, you bet I was, and I didn't feel one bit guilty about it.

The first cab off the rank was my GP. He was as shocked and upset as we were; two of my sisters work with him in a local medical centre and he knew how much our family had already been through. He also knew the severity of my diagnosis: the concern was written all over his face and we could hear it in his voice. He referred us to an oncologist. Apparently this doctor had recently changed his career path from obstetrics to oncology. *What an idiot!* Why would you swap bringing beautiful little innocent babies into the world for telling people they are on their way out?

He also gave us a referral for a biopsy to find out the strain of the cancer. That was what I had to look forward to the next day. Scott had work to do – he was a one-man-band and no one else could do it for him – so my beautiful dad offered to take me to that appointment and I reluctantly agreed. He wasn't my husband but he was the next best thing. I knew I wouldn't find out the results on that day so it was just another shitty thing that I had to do – tests, tests and more tests.

Thank goodness I didn't really know beforehand what the full extent of a biopsy was or how it was performed, because it was bloody horrible. I had to lie down while a radiographer stuck a needle into my liver. I was lying there in agony, tears flowing, just wanting to die right there and then. This was my worst nightmare and it had only just begun.

When it was over I walked back into the waiting room and sat down next to my dad. He didn't say anything, he just put his arm around me and pulled me close to his chest. The sadness was written all over his face.

I wanted my mum more than ever. But I couldn't have her. She wasn't on earth anymore. Maybe I was going to see her again sooner than I thought.

Somehow I lived through that procedure. The radiographer told us he would send the results to my doctor, the oncologist I was yet to meet. It would take two days, another excruciating bout of waiting. In the meantime I was walking around with a brain tumour along with several other tumours in my body.

What would they be doing in there? Not sitting around doing nothing, I was guessing. Probably having an absolute field day and there wasn't a thing I could do about it. I can't describe how unnerving that felt.

It was a few days before we could get an appointment with the oncologist. The waiting was killing us; we were still in the dark about what cancer we were dealing with so we had no idea what treatment, if any, was available. The thought of chemotherapy sickened me to the bone; I had seen my mother and sister go through it. I watched them feel awful, look awful, lose their hair and that was just the start. I was pretty sure chemotherapy would be offered to me, but I would have to think long and hard before going down that path.

Appointment day with the oncologist arrived: Thursday, just four days into the week and my third medical appointment. It had been just seven days since the seizure.

Oncologist. I hate that word. Almost as much as I hate the word *cancer.* I've always felt sorry for people who have Cancer as their star sign. The word just makes me anxious, but somehow I knew I would have to make peace with it.

Okay, so what do you wear to an oncologist appointment? I love fashion; my sisters and mother would tease me that I had an 'outfit for every occasion'. However this was one occasion for which I did not have an outfit. I kept it simple, a pair of jeans, long black boots, a black jumper and a bright orange scarf.

I remember thinking that I didn't feel sick, so why the hell should I have to dress like it.

That day I decided I would always dress stylishly, in happy, bright colours, and not like a cancer patient. If I was on my way out then I was going out in style.

Scott and I got into the car and we pulled out of the driveway. Once again, life was going on around us as per normal, like nothing had changed. It was winter and chilly but the sun was shining. There were people out and about, running, walking, chatting, having lunch, coffee, but we were on our way to hear my fate from a cancer doctor.

I was pissed off. I didn't want this life. I wanted their life! The people I was observing seemingly didn't have a worry in the world.

I stared out the window at the ocean as we drove. It was turbulent that day, as if mirroring my thoughts, our thoughts.

What am I in for?

What is the doctor going to tell us?

I looked across at Scott in the driver's seat; he was pissed off, too, I could tell. Like me, I'm guessing he wanted to be one of those couples having a lunch date in a restaurant on the beach, not on our date with destiny.

The oncologist's room was in a cold, dark, spooky wing of the hospital. This particular hospital is old, circa 1896, and renowned for its mental health facility in the east wing. I actually wished I was going to that facility so they could tell me I had conjured this whole thing up and offer me shock treatment.

No such luck, it was the oncology department for me! We parked the car, climbed the stairs slowly, checked in and sat down to wait. Scott and I didn't speak; we just sat there holding hands, still in disbelief.

'Julie Randall,' the doctor called.

Boy, was I going to hear that called out a lot. I was scared. We looked up at him, then he smiled, god knows why, and ushered us into his room. We were just about to be told what type of cancer we were dealing with. It was terrifying.

We sat down, the doctor introduced himself and Scott shook his hand. I didn't want to. He said he had the biopsy results.

Please say it's all been a big mistake, please Doc, please.

'You have melanoma,' he said rather calmly. The only part I liked about that was it didn't have the word 'cancer' in it.

With that, he said, 'I think this is a good thing, as they have a pill now that melts it all away.' I am not kidding – that is what he said, verbatim.

Did we hear him right? We were ecstatic, we hugged and cried. We were so happy. Perplexed, but happy. But of course it wasn't going to be that simple. He referred me to a professor at a specialist institute. I was completely baffled, though; I have fair skin and have always been diligent about my skin checks, so how the hell did I get melanoma? I explained this to him and he told me that sometimes with melanoma there is no primary site. So it wouldn't have mattered if I had a skin check on the morning of the seizure. It still would have happened.

We drove home that afternoon with hope in our hearts, so desperately wanting to believe everything was going to be okay. A pill that 'melted it all away' sounded a little bizarre but we were running with it. We stopped and picked up some champagne and the family came over to celebrate.

My brother and sisters, my father and our girls all sat on our back deck with the outdoor heaters on. Scott threw some kebabs on the barbecue and we talked and laughed. We rehashed old stories from our childhood and for the first time since this whole debacle had begun I could go for up to five minutes without thinking about cancer. Somewhere in the back corner of my mind it did seem a little irrational and absurd that this could all be melted away like an ice cream on a hot summer's day, but I wanted to believe in it more than anything I'd ever believed in before.

The appointment with the melanoma professor was at a hospital in the western suburbs, over an hour's drive away. My appointment was at 9am so we got up early to beat the traffic. It was July and the wind was icy.

Sticking to my word, I put on a pair of trendy black jeans my girls had given me for my birthday, high waisted with a slight shine to them. I put on a cream roll neck jumper and a black jacket. I added some colour with a long, pink beaded cross around my neck. If I looked good and felt good then surely I was going to be okay.

I glanced in the mirror, wishing I was going to work. I would wear this outfit to work, I mused.

Why can't I just go back to work like before? If I could just go back to that life, I would never complain about working again.

I was still on steroids and wasn't allowed to drive as there was still a risk of seizures, plus I wasn't capable of concentrating on a task for more than five minutes, so how could I go to work and perform my job as a membership coordinator at Marine Rescue New South Wales?

After a long, boring drive we arrived at the hospital. I didn't know what to feel, besides numb. I was already sick of doctors and the smell of hospitals. What was today going to bring? Would I be getting this magic pill to make me all better? God I hoped so.

Would this be it? Would the professor say, *Here you go, here're your pills, nothing to see here, bye bye*?

We were shown into the professor's room with three chairs, a basin in the corner and an examination bed, and told to take a seat, the professor would be with us shortly.

Just like my local hospital it was an old, cold building full of sick people and the room reflected that aura. Then she walked in, this striking woman with beautiful, flawless pale skin, her curly auburn hair tied up in a bun. She shook our hands. I smiled, I was happy to meet her because after all she was going to give me the good news, the hope, the magic pill, right?

She sat down and without hesitation said, 'Julie, you have stage four advanced metastatic melanoma and there is no cure for what you have, I'm very sorry.'

With that I stood up walked across the room and uncontrollably dry-retched into the basin in the corner. All I could mutter was, 'My babies, my babies, my babies.'

This was it, we had the news. There was no cure. I was going to die.

I wanted my mum.

Scott and the professor walked over and took an arm on either side of me to help me back to my seat. But I wanted the floor to open up and swallow me whole. I didn't want to sit back down on that chair and listen to my fate. Time stood still, I was suspended in that moment. *This wasn't happening, it couldn't be.*

Scott managed to say to her that my oncologist had told us there was a pill that melted it all away, that I would be okay. He said it over and over again, but I was taking nothing in.

Scott later told me that she said the pill was only for a specific gene mutation called BRAF that only occurs in a small number of patients and she didn't think I would be a candidate for it, but she would do the testing to make sure.

So there it was, once again in only two weeks, our world had come tumbling down. Unlike the other times, though, this time we knew for sure. I had a terminal illness; it was now a fact.

The words 'life expectancy' were being thrown around a lot. I didn't like her now; how could she sit there and tell me and Scott those things?

I had never met this woman and her opening line was, 'Sorry babe, you're gonna die.'

Well, not in those words but it certainly felt like it. I didn't like her offsider, either, who started talking about palliative care. Palliative fucking care. I didn't even feel sick.

I put my hand up in front of my face gesturing for her to stop; I couldn't take any more.

Among all of this chaos, apparently the doctor was talking about chemotherapy and another drug on the market, both with ten to fifteen per cent chance of response, albeit short term. That drug cost $120,000 and could cause extreme side effects such as Crohn's Disease, bowel blockages and other revolting conditions.

By that stage I had lost the plot. She must have been acutely aware of this, as she directed all of the conversation to Scott. Then finally she referred us to a brain surgeon, Doctor Brian Miller.

I already hated him, too, but apparently he was 'very good'. I was so glad to hear he wasn't just 'okay'.

I soon began to hate everyone who wasn't telling me something I wanted to hear. I know it sounds irrational, but that's just the way it was.

Suddenly it was urgent to have the brain tumour removed and she made us an appointment for the next day. Her sidekick asked me to go with her into another room to get some blood tests and have my weight checked. I politely declined. I couldn't face it. A bad reading on the scales was all I needed that morning. Don't laugh, it did cross my mind.

Scott and I left the room and walked down the hallway of that gloomy hospital all the way back to the car. It was an out-of-body experience. I had just heard the most horrible words anyone had ever said to me in my entire life. 'There is no cure for what you've got. You're dying.'

Before this day there was at least hope and now even the hope had been ripped away. We had to line up and pay for the parking; it was torture. I just wanted to get as far away from that place as I possibly could.

We got in the car and for the first time since this whole thing had started Scott lost the plot; he was crying and cursing and finally came out with the statement, 'And I worry about odd socks.'

I remember thinking that was a weird comment even under the circumstances, but he can be a little strange sometimes. So, once again, we were driving home from a gloomy old hospital with terrible news. We were beyond devastated.

I stared out the window. I was gutted.

'So much for the magic pill that's going to fix me,' I blurted out. I wanted to kill that doctor. I hated him, too, just as much as the rest of them. How could he give us such false hope?

But in a strange way I was glad I'd had that hope, even if it was short lived. Spending those precious moments with my family believing I was going to be okay had been a relief. Scott reminded me I was going to be tested to see if I was a candidate for the 'magic pill'. The professor had made it quite clear she didn't think I would be. She seemed pretty sure about that. I guess it was a tiny glimmer of hope we could hang on to but I wouldn't get my hopes up this time just to have them crushed again.

The one and a half hour drive back was excruciating. Scott kept rubbing my leg with his left hand. I looked down and saw his wedding ring firmly placed on his finger. God I was glad I had him right now. He didn't say much, he didn't need to. Nothing was going to change my reality. He couldn't say, 'You'll be right darl' like he normally did. There was nothing he could say to soften the blow of the metaphoric axe that had just been driven into my skull.

I guess about fifteen minutes of the trip home had passed when I started my rant.

'Please don't put me in the ground! I'm claustrophobic. Make sure you don't. And don't put me in one of those black funeral cars either. I hate them, they're so horrible, and I don't want you or the girls getting in one. Don't let any old balding men carry me into the church and I don't want people wearing black. And I will pick the outfit you put me in,'

I hadn't finished. 'I love you and I want you to be happy, so you have my permission to meet someone else and move on with your life.'

Then something snapped inside me: the green-eyed monster appeared and I suddenly changed my mind. 'I take that back, it's not going to happen,' I said through my streaming tears. I had a renewed determination. The thought of him, my husband, my lover, my favourite person in the universe, cosying up with another woman made me feel sicker than the stage four metastatic melanoma with NO CURE.

In that moment I decided I was going to do whatever I could, whatever it took, to find a way through this.

It was going to be the toughest journey of my life, but I was going to do it. I wanted to be with my kids for a lot longer and I would be damned if I was going to have my husband parading around town with another woman on his arm.

I imagined a younger, hotter woman by his side and it cut me like a knife.

I was adamant: it just wasn't going to happen. Then the reality of my condition washed over me. Maybe I wouldn't be here to stop it.

Chapter Five

So again we gathered with family. This time we headed straight to my sister Michelle's house. Scott and I were completely shattered.

A big part of me was determined to get through this ordeal, but another part was terrified. When we walked in I was crying . . . for a change. It was surprising I had any tears left.

It was surreal. I felt absolutely normal physically, but had been given a life expectancy of what, days, weeks, months? I'm still not sure, my brain wouldn't let me take that in at the time. Scott knows what she said but has never told me. I've since looked it up and apparently I had six to twelve months to live!

Dad was sad and sombre but my sister Michelle as always wouldn't accept the prognosis. She grabbed my face with both her hands, looked me right in the eyes and said, 'We will get through this.' She had been through so much herself and it pained me to put yet another burden on her. She's a very strong woman, though, and I knew I could count on her for absolutely anything.

I really wanted to believe her words. I was crying so much that I didn't even bother to try to blow my nose anymore. I didn't care what I looked like. I just wanted to get up and run, run so far away from myself that I couldn't be found. But this was the one and only thing I couldn't run away from. I was stuck with me and the harrowing thoughts going round and round in my head.

Scott just sat there with a sad, incredulous look on his face. Then, after an uncomfortable silence, through tears I told them all I was going to find a way through this, I would do whatever it took to give myself the best chance of survival. I'd promised my girls I would fix this, and I had to keep my promise. My head was spinning and my thoughts were going crazy, jumping from one thing to another. The diagnosis, the treatment, the brain surgery . . . my mind just wouldn't stop. Would I be the same after the surgery? Would I be normal? Would I be a dribbling disabled person in the corner at family gatherings?

I knew my speech had gone when I had the seizure and I feared that would happen again, but this time for good. How could I navigate my way through this minefield without my full brain capacity?

Getting through this surgery with my mind intact was just the first step. I had to break this situation down and deal with one thing at a time. It was so hard not to jump ahead and think of all the horrible things I was in for. That we were *all* in for.

My poor family, why am I putting them through all of this again? I was overcome with guilt. This was all my fault. Then momentarily I was out of my body looking down at me, the woman in the chair. *You poor little girl, you need your mummy.* I felt sorry for her.

'Do you want a cup of tea?' someone asked, interrupting my thoughts.

It wasn't even midday and I remember responding, 'No thanks, I'll have a beer.'

I ended up having a few beers that day; I figured I was in enough trouble, surely a beer or three wasn't going to make things any worse. The rest of the day was a blur. I was exhausted and this was only the beginning.

Scott and I went home to the girls but I didn't tell them anything about what had been said that day. How could I tell them that I had a terminal illness? I couldn't, I wouldn't. I was sticking to the game plan. I was going to fix this no matter what. How? I didn't know, but I was filled with resolve.

For now, we just told them we had to go to see the brain surgeon the next day and organise to get the tumour removed. That was a scary concept for them. They already had enough crap to deal with. I would not terrify them with any more.

I cried myself to sleep that night. Why the hell was this happening? What did my family do to deserve this?

Then I woke up staring into the darkness wondering what my husband was thinking. I felt so bad for him. Bad that he married me and had to deal with this nightmare. I was going through our marriage vows in my head. *For better or for worse, in sickness and in health, for richer for poorer, till death do us part.*

Every one of these vows would be tested to the extreme. The last one maybe a little sooner than expected. I cuddled up to him, loving him so much and knowing he would be there for me no matter how tough it got.

After a sleepless night we were off to see the brain surgeon. I wanted to look extra bright, healthy and alive that day, so I wore a lime-green sweater with black jeans and boots and a multi-coloured scarf. I applied make-up and wore lip gloss. I didn't want to look like a cancer patient, especially one with a brain tumour. I didn't know exactly what they looked like, but they didn't look like me.

We drove across the Harbour Bridge to the inner city. It was a sunny Sydney day but extremely windy, I remember my hair blowing all over the place on the way up the street towards Doctor Miller's rooms. Not wanting to look dishevelled, I stopped and brushed it before we went into the building.

Being a brain surgeon is obviously a lucrative occupation because in total contrast to all of the previous appointments we had endured, this building was new and bright with plenty of colourful artwork on the walls and stylish leather furniture in the waiting room. It was a pleasant change, I thought, as if that was going to make a difference to the outcome. We checked in and sat down for the usual wait.

And then it came, 'Julie Randall?'

So, up we got, off the stylish leather sofas and walked reluctantly into the doctor's room. We were taken aback, it was the same doctor from St Vincent's, the one who stood at the foot of my bed with the interns on that horrendous Friday night. The short, stocky guy with the buzz cut. He would be the man to remove the malignant tumour from my brain. I promptly made the decision that it was in my best interest not to hate him anymore.

'You look well,' Doctor Miller said with a surprised look on his face.

Little did he know I had made a huge effort to look as good as I was feeling. Psychologically I was a basketcase, but physically I felt great. Sadly that didn't mean I was well, not on the inside anyway.

He put my X-rays up on a light box and said, 'Okay, I think I can get this out without too much damage. But there is always a risk of complications. The tumour is about the size of a marble and it's in the lower left temporal lobe.'

Scott and I sat and listened. I relied on him to remember more details than me, which was ironic as I was always telling him he had CRAFT disease. I will let you work out what this acronym stands for.

Brian the Brain Surgeon went on to say without too much expression, 'Go home, pack your bags and be at the hospital in two hours. You can get all the pre-op stuff done today and I will operate in the morning.'

I was having brain surgery in the morning. I couldn't believe this was happening to me. But it was.

I didn't ask too many questions. It was what it was and the tumour had to come out. I didn't dare ask what he meant by 'not too much damage'; I trusted he would do his best to preserve the rest of my brain and that had to be enough for now.

We drove home, I packed my bags and off we went again. I was scared, Scott was scared, but obviously trying to stay calm for my sake.

It was incomprehensible. Just a little over two weeks earlier I'd been dancing up a storm in a sexy bright-green mini dress at my 50th birthday party with all my amazing family and friends. I'd called it a black and white party, but I wanted to be the belle of the ball so I chose the most colourful dress I could find.

It took me ages to look at those photos and I still haven't watched the video. It's just too hard. To think about what happened just five days later is beyond difficult, it's impossible. You just never know, you never ever know what can happen in a single moment that can change your life forever.

That afternoon on the way to the hospital I made a pact with the universe that went something like this: 'If I get through this, Mrs Universe, I will never take life for granted again. I will do everything I've ever said I would do. I will not put things off. I will be a doer, not a "gonna do". I will have fun at every turn. I will love more, dance more, sing more, help more. I will launch my blog. I will write that book . . .' The list went on.

I've always wanted to write but I didn't know what the hell to write about. *Maybe I have something now*, I thought. I'd heard the saying 'life is short' a thousand times, but it had just bitten me right on the arse and I had no choice but to stand up and take notice. If I get through this, I promised the universe I would never be a 'gonna' again.

We arrived at the hospital in two hours as instructed. The place was nice as far as hospitals go. Scott did all the paperwork. I couldn't face it. I was in a whole new world of my own, but not in a good way.

'How the hell did I get here?' I kept saying over and over.

The next hurdle: another MRI scan and as I've said, I hate them. I'm claustrophobic and they are my worst nightmare. Well, part of my worst nightmare, anyway. I just couldn't do it. After three failed attempts and behaviour that can only be described as childish, they finally let Scott in to hold my leg and talk me through it again. This MRI had to be done as Brian the Brain Surgeon needed a 'marker scan' so he could navigate his way around my brain to check how much the tumour had grown since my previous MRI. With Scott's help I managed to get through it.

Then came all the other pre-op tests. Scott stayed with me that afternoon as long as he could. I wanted him there all night in bed next to me but he had to go home to our girls.

There I was, alone again in a hospital with only my thoughts for company and, unsurprisingly, not very nice ones. I knew a couple of people who were not completely the same after brain surgery. One has since passed away and the other is a little different than she used to be.

The thought process was surreal. Could this be the last few hours of me? Me as I know me. Me as my husband knows me.

Me as my girls know me. Me as my family and friends know me. I knew my husband was wrestling with the same thoughts.

Doctor Brian said he could remove the tumour 'without too much damage' but we had no idea what that meant. This was the scariest thing I had ever been through. I lay there in disbelief, frozen with fear and crippled with guilt for putting my family through this nightmare.

I asked the nurse for a sleeping pill and she obliged. I called Scott and the girls to say goodnight, hoping this wasn't my final goodbye. Then I lay there, waiting for sleep to come. I just wanted the operation to be over. I couldn't handle the horrible thoughts anymore and I wanted this thing out of my head. I somehow managed to drift off but not for long. Then I lay in my dark new world, scared and alone, for as long as I could handle it before buzzing for some more pills. Again I drifted off.

I was roused from my sleep with a hand gently rubbing my arm. It was my husband, he was back, he didn't want me to wake up alone. It was very early in the morning and still dark. We made small talk. He pulled back the covers and snuggled in next to me. I managed to have a joke with him about hiding under the blanket and sneaking into the operating theatre.

'I would if I could,' he whispered.

I cuddled him and could feel his heart beating fast.

I couldn't eat or drink because of my imminent operation, not that I felt like it, but my mouth was dry and I needed water. Scott got me some ice to suck on. I lay there and I looked up at him, imagining the situation in reverse. I would hate it with every bone in my body. I would want to take his place. I was glad it was me and not him, and I remember being weirdly comforted by that thought.

A short time later Doctor Brian appeared; I was secretly hoping he had called in sick but no such luck. There he was right in front of me, the man who was just about to cut my head open and remove a malignant tumour from my brain. On one hand I wanted it out, on the other I still wanted to be me.

I looked down at his stumpy little fingers and hoped he had good dexterity. He went over the procedure in detail but to be honest I didn't want to know the details.

Just do it, I was thinking.

Then within a minute, the nurse appeared with a burly young orderly whose job was to wheel me to the operating theatre.

So this is it, it's happening.

It felt like I was on death row and being transported to the execution room. They wheeled me into the lift and down to the first floor to prepare for theatre.

The tears started streaming. Thinking of my girls, I turned to Scott. 'Tell Morgan and Remy I love them so much it hurts and if something happens to me I want them to live their lives to the fullest.' I begged him, my heart breaking, the emotions and feelings frightening me that I may never see them again.

I wanted my mum.

I looked up at him; he had tears rolling down his cheeks. He leaned down and kissed me, then whispered in my ear, 'I love you so much.' Then the big double doors of the operation room swung open and I was gone.

As I came to I could see Scott's face; he was gingerly stroking my head.

I was in the Intensive Care Unit (ICU) with tubes, monitors and god knows what else attached to me. Then Brian the Brain Surgeon popped in with his white surgical cap on and said, 'It all went well.'

He asked me my name, date of birth and what day it was. I very slowly answered and got two out of three correct. I had no idea what day it was!

'Not bad,' he joked.

My memory was almost intact. Part of me wished it wasn't, as the hard times were far from over and forgetting all of this would have been a blessing.

Doctor Brian went on to say that the tumour looked like melanoma, as if to confirm the diagnosis we had already been given.

'Oh, and you have sixteen staples in your head,' he said matter-of-factly as he left the ICU, followed by, 'I'll come and see you tomorrow.'

Scott stayed as long as he could, then I sent him home to be with the girls. Seeing me like that would have been gut-wrenching for him. Then the pain came with a vengeance as the anaesthetic wore off and the next 24 hours were what I can only describe as hell on earth.

I didn't have one of those self-administering drug devices, so I had to buzz every time I needed a top-up. I wanted to buzz

Julie Randall

every five minutes but tried to hold out as long as I could. I had a beautiful nurse called Alyssa who rubbed my hand gently and smiled at me while never questioning my excessive drug use.

The whole time I lay there going through different levels of intense pain, still trying to process what was happening to me. In a little over two weeks I had turned 50, had a seizure, been told I had stage four advanced cancer with no cure, had a brain tumour removed and was now in ICU with sixteen staples in my head.

I became inconsolable; this was *Nightmare on Elm Street* personified. And then came GWEN . . . My beautiful nurse Alyssa kissed my bandage goodnight. 'I'll see you tomorrow,' she said softly.

'Hello, I'm Gwen,' said the silver-haired, 60-something nurse I later discovered had been called in from a temp agency. She fussed about checking monitors, taking blood pressure, shoving thermometers under my tongue, fiddling with buttons and then she curtly asked, 'What's your pain level from one to ten?'

What pain would that be, Gwen? I felt like saying. *The pain that my children might not have a mother? The pain that my husband may lose his wife? The pain that I may not live to witness my daughters get married or see my grandchildren? Or the physical pain that pales into insignificance in comparison?*

'Ten,' I said, 'please give me more painkillers.'

'Are you sure it's a ten?' she asked. She was not endearing herself to me from the start.

'Ten,' I raised my voice. 'Yes, TEN.' This was going to be a very, very long night.

There was no chance of sleep, the left side of my head felt like someone had hit me with an axe and the axe was still embedded in my skull. *You'd better not be scrimping me on the morphine Gwen*, I thought. *You don't know who you're messing with. I can be very feisty and for some reason I am not in a very good mood.*

I lay there waiting it out but then enough was enough. I buzzed again, and in she came with an annoyed look on her face.

'What's your pain level from . . .'

'Ten,' I said before she could say another word.

'But it was ten before and I've given you more morphine,' she said.

So with that I picked up my right arm and motioned with my pointer finger for her to come closer to me. She obeyed.

'Listen Gwen,' I said softly, 'I have just had my world turned upside down and apparently I have an incurable disease. I have just had a brain tumour removed from my head and it has been put back together with sixteen staples. Now if I say my pain is a ten, Gwen, then it is a ten and if I say I want more drugs, Gwen, then please give me more drugs.'

She walked away and didn't ask me about my pain levels for the rest of the night. I buzzed, she administered. Finally Gwen and I were on the same page.

After a long, tedious night with no sleep, Gwen was gone and Alyssa was back. 'I love you,' I said as she walked through the door.

She smiled, looking a little perplexed. I told her about Gwen and she was genuinely upset for me. She told me to report her, so I did. I didn't want anyone else to go through that horror on top of whatever else they were dealing with. If you're in ICU chances are you're not in your 'happy place', and do not need any further aggravation.

Alyssa arranged to have me transferred to the ward. The same orderly wheeled me there. Alyssa came along to settle me in and brief my new nurse. The room was lovely, more like a hotel than a hospital room – the advantages of a private hospital – and again it was a beautiful, sunny winter's day. It was a big room and I had it all to myself. I had a city view from my bed and I like to look outside; I hate feeling confined.

I was staring out the window and my mind briefly wandered back to a time when Scott surprised me with a romantic getaway. We both love music and love the Basement at Sydney's Circular Quay. A funky place with timber floors and railings with really cool R&B bands playing, it was our special place. He'd bought tickets to see a band, booked a hotel room with stunning harbour views, we drank champagne, fooled around, then wandered down to the Opera Bar to have dinner before the show. It was during Vivid Sydney. If you haven't seen Vivid, it is a light, music and ideas festival where unique images and colours are reflected onto the buildings at night, and various events take place throughout the city. It's so bright and colourful and creates an amazing atmosphere.

I was thinking how lucky I was to have had the perfect marriage. We love hard, we fight hard – we fight over everything and anything, big and small. We don't talk for days here and there when one of us has really pissed the other one off. We have two gorgeous daughters we made all by ourselves, a house and a dog. To me that's perfection.

Just when I began to lose myself in that beautiful memory, I snapped back to reality. I was back in the room.

I'd asked the nurse to bring me a mirror as I wanted to see my head. The pain seemed to be under control so at least I had something to be happy about. As she handed it to me I raised the mirror and slowly brought it up to my face. Who was I looking at?

My face was bloodied, bruised and I had a bandage wrapped around my head. I looked very similar to a front-row Rugby player. Dried blood everywhere, it was like something out of a horror movie. I cried. Was this really me?

Life can be cruel sometimes, I thought, but I was grateful that I felt sort of normal, well, the new normal, anyway. Maybe my brain was still intact. As I put down the mirror my dad and brother walked in, both with very solemn faces. I started shaking.

'What's happening to me?' I asked them as if they had the answers.

'I want Mum, I need her,' I said to my dad.

'I know, darling,' he said, 'I know.' He held me tightly while my brother stood in the background with his head down. He didn't speak; what could he say?

My mum had died a little over ten years earlier on her 66th birthday and we all still missed her and we all needed her now more than ever.

Then in the middle of my tearful embrace with my dad, I got a text from Scott saying he and the girls were on their way up from the carpark. Feeling sorry for myself was soon replaced with snapping into action, drying my tears, splashing my face and trying to be semi-okay when my girls walked into the room. Dad and my brother said goodbye and left me alone with my little family.

I loved seeing Scott and the girls but hated that they had to see me in that state. Although we did manage to have a joke about me looking like a footballer with one of those silly headbands that protects them from getting cauliflower ears. We chatted for about an hour and I managed to keep my brave face on before sending them home to normality. Those three are my world.

Chapter Six

Letter to Mum in Heaven

Hi Mum,

Where the hell are you? When are you coming home? I really need you right about NOW.

So, to borrow one of your favourite sayings, I have decided that . . . 'If Mohammed won't come to the mountain, the mountain will go to Mohammed!'

Well, my beautiful mother, the shit has really hit the fan down here. There is no easy way to tell you this, so, I'm just going to say it . . . I've been diagnosed with stage four advanced metastatic malignant melanoma, and they say there's no cure. I don't really understand the stage thing but apparently four's not too flash.

I'm scared Mum, really scared. I would love to be with you but I'm not ready. I have Scott and the girls and I have so much to do. I'm only 50, a young 50 and I want to stay here with my family, they need me. I'm not scared of dying, Mum. You said it yourself, 'Everyone has to go sometime,' but not yet, Mum, not now!

I can't leave them behind with a hole in their hearts that never mends like the hole you left in my heart, in all of our hearts.

I look for you all the time. I squint and look for you in the moon. I stare at the clouds and sometimes think I see the outline of your face. You said you would be looking down on us and you never, ever told us lies, so I believe you and I know you're out there somewhere. I have never doubted that.

I miss you so much, we all do. Part of our life ended on 26 February 2002 when you left us. It was your 66th birthday. I sang you a song that day. Do you remember, Mum? Your favourite song and only you and I know what it was.

Mum, I have everyone around me, but I feel so alone. Alone with my thoughts and feelings. No one can be in my mind with me and I can't run away from myself. There's a constant noise of uncertainty of what lies ahead.

We talk about you all the time and laugh about all the things you did and said. You were one of the funniest people who ever graced this universe.

The day you went away was the worst day of my life. I sat on our back deck trying to fathom what had happened;

you were gone. *Gone forever. I was just sitting there staring into the night and the biggest white eagle you have ever seen flew across the backyard, flying as low as you can imagine to make sure I noticed it. Its enormous wings were flapping but it was like slow motion. I know it was you, Mum. It was majestic.*

I'm in a bit of trouble right now but I have promised my girls I am going to find a way through this. As much as I would love to be with you up there, out there, wherever you are, I can't right now. Please help me, Mum. Can you put in a good word with the big guy upstairs for me? Is there one? And if there is, surely all those years of going to Sunday Mass and listening to boring sermons and eating white cardboard cut in circles that stuck to my tongue has to account for something.

I love you and wish you were here with me to tell me everything will be okay. I need you.

I miss you so much,
Jule

Chapter Seven

My three sisters came into my hospital room that night with smiling faces and they smuggled in a Corona for me. They had even cut up a lime to pop in, god love them. As per our 'normal' life, they figured having a beer together fixed everything.

So there I was, propped up in bed looking like Freddy Krueger with my beautiful sisters having a beer, just like everything was the same as before. The nurse walked in and did a double take, then smirked and walked back out. She knew my story and she wasn't going to rain on my parade. I loved her for that.

We talked and laughed and they did everything in their power to distract me from the enormity of my situation. It worked. We talked about Mum and the funny things she used to do and say. We all wished she were here on earth right now, although no one said the words because we knew what would happen. The floodgates would open and we would all fall apart.

I really loved having my sisters there with me. I know they would have stayed all night if they could, but they couldn't. The hospital didn't allow three grown women sleeping on the floor, as harsh as that seems. The time came, they had to go, so one by one they kissed me goodbye. I tried so hard not to cry. My heart ached for them as I knew the hell they were going through seeing me in that state.

Tears are rolling down my face as I write this because I've walked a mile in their shoes; I had watched people I love go through horrific times and it dragged at my heart so much that at times I thought it would just stop and I would die.

I felt dead inside watching the people I love suffer. I knew my sisters were putting on sunny faces for me and that when they left the room their mood would change. They would be distraught.

They were gone and I was alone again in that big room with my big ugly thoughts about the future. I was desperately trying to convince myself I would find my way back home, back to the way things were. Me, Scott and the girls and Roxy our dog, our beautiful golden retriever, just doing the family thing, living normal lives. It was hard to be logical. I had to remind myself, *One step at a time, Julie*, but there was also urgency about my condition. This thing was fast moving, the oncologist had said; I couldn't just hit the pause button.

Reconciling all those thoughts was messy and confusing. I don't know how I stayed sane. Mum always said we were all too crazy to go insane.

The nurse came in to do the usual observation stuff and offered me a sleeping pill. I accepted without hesitation. From past experience I knew it would help me sleep, even if it was only a few hours. Just a few short hours of sleep, then I lay awake from 2am trying to sing songs in my head to distract me from my gloomy thoughts.

Don McLean's 'American Pie' was the longest song I knew, so if I could challenge myself with all the verses then that would at least kill ten minutes. I remembered the first line, then the second, then the rest of the verse and the chorus. My memory seemed to be intact! I was still remembering the words to songs, that was something, right? I sang every verse in my head word for word right to the end.

Singing about 'the day the music died' and the closing words about this being 'the day that I die' were obviously not ideal. *Great song choice!* I thought to myself.

Was I going to die? I was desperate for some happy news, but when would that be? I had no idea if I would ever get happy news again.

I didn't want to die, not this day, not this year, not for a bloody long time. I am a life lover, I love people and people love me. I'm the one at parties playing all the music; renowned for knowing all the words. I systematically listed every song for the DJ at our wedding and my 50th birthday just three weeks earlier. Everyone was having the best time. The dance floor was packed till 3am. The music will never die for me.

I had to find a way to live.

The tears flowed freely in the darkness in that hospital bed; I didn't try to wipe them, they just dried on their own.

I somehow made it through the long, awful night and was listening out for the food trolley which would have a cup of tea onboard. I was craving that cup of tea! I heard footsteps approaching my room at the end of the corridor but it wasn't my tea, it was Brian the Brain Surgeon.

'Hi Julie, how are you feeling?' he asked in an upbeat voice.

Apart from gutted, devastated, confused and scared I was feeling fine, so that's what I said. He seemed rather shocked at how well I was and how well I could communicate.

'Been eating and drinking okay?'

'Yep, all good,' I replied. I failed to mention chugging down a Corona the night before.

'You know what?' he said. 'You're doing really well so, you can go home today. I'll get my secretary to call you and make an appointment for a follow-up. Oh and you will need to see the radiation oncologist to schedule radiation to the site where the tumour was removed.'

'Fabulous, that sounds like fun,' I said.

He just looked at me, perplexed. Then I felt bad, it wasn't his fault I was in this position and let's not forget he had just successfully removed a tumour from my brain without too much damage, just as he'd promised.

He was a clever man and I did feel grateful. I'm not an arrogant person by nature although some may say otherwise. I was just taking my frustrations out on him. I'm pretty sure he understood that.

He left and my cuppa arrived. Thank goodness for small mercies.

I was glad to be going home, I wanted to be with my family and just be, well, some kind of normal. I was on a cocktail of drugs – steroids, painkillers, blood thinners, sleeping pills – that culminated in making me feel a little emotional, strangely enough, but I had to get home and get on with it.

Home was where I needed to be. My darling husband came for me around lunchtime and the nurse did all the final checks – blood pressure, temperature, pupils, etc.

The last thing she said to me as I left was, 'Goodbye and I don't want to see you back here again.'

She was an attractive woman about my age and I liked her. I knew what she meant and in an inexplicable way I felt she believed in me. She knew that my condition never ended well, but I also got the sense that she saw something in me. I don't remember her name but we connected. Her words meant the world to me.

It was a relief to be going home, where I could pretend, if only for 60 seconds, that things were normal. We all knew they weren't, but we would try.

My diary was going to be full, but not like the appointment book from my previous life. There would be no 10.15am gym, 1.30pm lunch with the girls, 6.30pm touch training, along with my work. This timetable was going to be entirely different, more like: 11.30am radio oncology, 2.30pm oncologist, 4pm melanoma professor, 4.45pm CT scan, 5.30pm MRI. Not a great schedule.

It was a Friday afternoon and Roxy greeted us at the door performing her usual little welcome-home dance. I was happy my girls had plans for that night. They were going out with their friends and I encouraged them to enjoy themselves. The thought of them being normal teenagers, getting dressed up and having fun filled my heart. I also felt comfort knowing they had their boyfriends to lean on, although I found out later some boys just don't get it. I think I already knew that.

After trying to eat some dinner I sat on the sofa staring at the TV screen, taking absolutely nothing in. We decided to go up to bed. Scott administered my painkilling drugs and sleeping pills as instructed by the nurse and they seemed to do the trick.

Just for that night, though. The next morning came with excruciating pain. I wasn't expecting this – it took me by surprise. My thoughts went back to Gwen in the ICU. My pain level had now become an eleven. It felt like every single one of the sixteen staples in my head was burning into my skull. I tried to hold it together but the pain became intense and even the heaviest of drugs weren't doing a thing to ease it.

Scott was distraught and didn't know what to do. Around 11am he bundled me into the car and took me to the medical centre where two of my sisters worked. We were very well known there and I could see the look of sadness, compassion and pity on the faces of everyone who was on duty. That look would soon become very familiar.

It was horrible coping with the pity on top of everything else. I broke down sobbing in front of Judy the on-duty nurse and she cuddled me *and* Scott. She was lovely. She gave me an injection and the pain finally subsided. We returned home and even managed to take Roxy for a very short walk up to the beach that afternoon. That dog was my best friend, she didn't say much, she didn't have to, she just knew. She was beside me every step of the way.

The next day was Sunday. I asked Scott, 'What's next?'

He'd been organising my appointment book while I was in hospital.

'Don't think about it until we have to,' he said.

'Well tomorrow's Monday, so I figure we have to.'

To make it as painless as possible we sat on our back deck overlooking the park with a cuppa and talked about our next steps.

'Tuesday morning you have a 10 o'clock appointment with the melanoma professor.'

My stomach sank when he told me that. A grim reminder that there was a lot more going on in my body that had to be dealt with.

'Wednesday you have one with the local oncologist, and we need to book into the radio oncologist too.'

I felt numb. It was like I had already been pushed to my limits and this was only the start.

Scott had spoken to Brian the Brain Surgeon, who had said I needed to book my radiation appointment as soon as possible, but first things first. Tuesday came and we set off for our appointment with the professor. Once again I took pride in my appearance. It was one of the few things I could control: I was determined not to look like a sick person who didn't give a damn about what they looked like as they'd be dead soon anyway.

Thankfully this appointment wasn't in the old, cold, creepy hospital. That was definitely a bonus. I was nervous and scared. I felt ill, actually, like I might throw up. We parked in the carpark below and caught the lift up to Level Two, the 'specialist' floor. We walked into the professor's suite, which was modern and bright, just like Brian's rooms. We checked in at reception, then sat quietly holding hands waiting for my name to be called, my foot tapping nervously on the ground. I was about to find out the treatment she would prescribe for the insidious disease I apparently had inside me.

I didn't want to see the professor again. She had given me such bad news last time; why would this situation be any better? She'd already told me there was no cure for my condition. What could she possibly say to put my mind at ease? She had told me she would test me for the BRAF but she didn't think that I had that mutation, and in any case my brain tumour had to be sent to Queensland for testing. That in itself seemed crazy. By the way, she was right, I was negative for the BRAF mutation and wasn't eligible for the supposed magic pill.

The waiting room was full of people much older than me and mostly men. I felt out of place. This all just seemed like a bad dream. We'd been sitting there for at least twenty minutes when I looked up and saw her. My stomach dropped. My body jerked. My heart leapt into my throat.

She looked just the same – attractive, perfectly groomed, wearing a beige knee-length sleeveless cotton dress, heels and her curly auburn hair tied up in a ponytail. Walking over to the tray at the end of the reception counter, she looked down and picked up a cream manila folder, then looked up and said the words, 'Julie Randall'.

I didn't want to get off my chair; Scott grabbed my arm and pulled me up. It wasn't that I wasn't capable, I just didn't bloody want to!

We followed her down the corridor to the office at the end. She had a female assistant with her but not the same woman as before. We sat down and she said, 'How are you after the surgery? You look well.'

I had made an effort, but this time I didn't feel so well. My head was still not quite right.

'I'm okay I guess,' I responded.

She explained that the only treatment available to me was a chemotherapy drug called Dacarbazine, which had a ten per cent chance of response and even if I responded well, this was never a cure. There it was again, the no cure thing. I felt like saying, 'Thank you Captain Obvious,' but I managed to bite my tongue. I hated hearing those words. They made me feel like I wanted to run, run away as fast and as far as I could.

This drug had many common side effects such as fatigue, nausea and vomiting, hair loss, too, but usually not full hair loss, just partial. Woohoo! And if I responded, the expected response and amount of time for stability wasn't long.

She informed me that apart from these treatments there were some clinical trials going on in Australia that were not available to us, but it was expected there would be more in the future, yet not for some time and nothing was a certainty. Time was something I didn't have. And if I started chemotherapy I would not be eligible for any of them anyway. The trials were called 'first line', which means you don't qualify unless you've had no treatment at all. I didn't have time to wait around. I did not want chemotherapy; I had seen what it does first hand, but I had to do something to slow down this thing until I could work out a plan of survival. My girls were at the forefront of my mind.

A ten per cent response rate was not great, but apparently this was my only option. Oh, apart from the drug we were told about at the first visit, which has a fifteen per cent chance of response and cost $120,000 Australian dollars for three injections with a huge chance of crippling side effects such as Crohn's Disease, bowel blockages and liver failure, which would be just marvellous on top of everything else.

The professor didn't think I should take the latter option.

How can life be so cruel? I was thinking; I had had an amazing life. I thought things like this happened to other people. Don't we all. But cancer doesn't discriminate! I just sat there staring at the floor.

Did I really want to go on a chemical therapy drug with such a low percentage of response? It would make me feel sick and revolting. Was that my only choice? I guess I had to. I didn't know what to think. In fact I didn't want to think at all. I had had enough and then something in my brain shut down. I wasn't crying, I wasn't devastated, I was numb.

The professor mentioned booking another appointment with the oncologist and that's where the chemo would be administered. She paused for my reaction and I mumbled something like, 'I'll think about it.'

It had been almost a month since I fell to the ground that day in the office and yet it felt like ten years.

Scott and I didn't talk on the way home. He could see that I was in zombie land and he let me stay there. He knew I wasn't up for a pep talk or even small talk for that matter. There's something about being so close to someone for 25 years. You learn when to talk and when to just shut the hell up.

Chapter Eight

Unfortunately my new normal was taking shape – Wednesday arrived with another trip to the oncologist. I wasn't looking forward to going back to the old hospital; in fact, I was dreading it. However I had decided that I owed it to my family to start some sort of treatment, so I had to go. My new life, it seemed, was filled with 'have-to'.

The doctor called us into his room and tried to make small talk, but I wasn't in the mood. I wanted to get down to the job at hand.

'Okay,' he said, 'so the professor has prescribed Dacarbazine, the chemotherapy drug that is used for patients with advanced melanoma.'

'Yes,' I said, 'and it has a ten per cent chance of response. We're not exactly thrilled about the odds.'

He nodded awkwardly, then went on to say that he'd heard about a chemo combination therapy at a conference in the USA using Abraxane (a breast cancer drug) and Pazopanib (a kidney cancer drug). It had been tested in a small clinical trial of 40 melanoma patients in Germany and around 35 per cent of the patients in the trial had responded. Some had even had extensive shrinkage of their tumours.

He explained it wasn't something readily available to patients in Australia, but if we agreed to use this option he could order the Pazopanib in for us and I could get started on the drugs.

The treatment would mean total hair loss and all the usual side effects that go with chemotherapy. This wasn't a surprise, I'd had a feeling I wouldn't get away with keeping my hair. Lady Luck was definitely not on my side.

Scott and I agreed that if chemo was our only option then we would go with the higher statistics. No-brainer, really! My oncologist said he would call the professor and discuss our preference with her. But he didn't want to tread on her toes!

Well I couldn't help myself; before I knew it, I blurted out that I didn't care whose effing toes he trod on, this was my life we were talking about. 'I have two children who need their mother,' I said, 'so if those drugs you mentioned have a better chance at prolonging my life, then just order them now. The only person's permission you need is mine.'

'Yes,' he said, 'of course. I will just give her a courtesy call.'

Scott didn't know which way to look. I didn't want to touch chemotherapy with a barge pole, but what could I do? I couldn't just sit around doing nothing, waiting for this thing to kill me.

I just needed to respond to a treatment long enough to get my head around how I was going to find a long-term solution that *apparently* didn't exist. Well, at least I had a 35 per cent chance of responding, which was far better than ten – I didn't have to be Einstein to work that out.

I was dreading the thought of feeling sick and watching my hair fall out in clumps. I loved my long blonde hair. I was born white-blonde and it had stayed that way all the way to 50. If I had a dollar for every time someone asked me what colour I used to get my hair that shade I would be a rich woman. Scott loved my hair. He would tell me what he loved about it the most, but I can't tell you what it was because it is just a little inappropriate!

Oh my god, why am I worrying about my hair?

Because it's a big deal for you, I responded to myself.

I had seen my mother and sister lose their hair and it wasn't nice at all. When I was with them I would put on a brave face, then walk away and cry my eyes out. 'They didn't ask for this,' I would say out loud. 'What on earth have they done to deserve this?' And *now* it was *my* turn.

We went home from the hospital that afternoon with a tiny bit of hope in our hearts. We just needed to do something to try to slow down this rampage of killer cells invading my body. It was the most hideous, unnerving feeling, that this invasion was happening right under my skin and I had no control over it.

That afternoon my phone rang. I didn't recognise the number so I hesitated to pick up, but something made me take the call.

'Hi Julie.' I didn't register the voice right away. Then she said her name.

'Oh, hi,' I said. It was the professor. She must have been speaking to me from somewhere outside because I could hear children playing in the background.

She'd started holidays that day and was with her children in the park. It was hard to imagine her being a normal person with children; to me, she was just a doctor and by now I'd been reading what a brilliant doctor she was from her online profile and that she had made it her life's work to find more effective treatments for melanoma.

'I've spoken to your oncologist and I'm happy for you to take the option of the combination therapy,' she went on to say. 'It's not something I can offer myself as it's still in the trial stages, but your oncologist is within his rights to prescribe it as he's an independent doctor.' Then came the bombshell. 'But this will not change your life expectancy.'

What she meant by that I don't know, but she might as well have put her fist through the phone and ripped out my insides. After trying to clear the lump in my throat, I actually said to her, 'Please don't say that to me, I just don't want to hear those words.'

She paused for a second, then said, 'Okay,' and she never mentioned those words to me again.

'Julie,' she said, 'I have seen a lot of melanoma patients, believe me, and I have never seen anyone looking as well as you at your stage of the disease.'

That would be the advanced metastatic melanoma stage four of the disease and I'm guessing it was supposed to be a compliment. At the time, though, it was very hard for me to take it that way. Apart from the horrible stuff, I really did appreciate her taking the time to call me during her holiday and I told her that. I realised that day that doctors can only offer you what is in their arsenal at the time, but there is a lot more going on with treatments and research in the world. I had never been great at homework but I knew that would have to change, and quick.

My oncologist kindly ordered the Pazopanib (the kidney cancer drug) for me. It was coming from a pharmaceutical company in Western Australia and would only take a few days, so he scheduled me in for my first infusion the following week. As much as I hated the thought of chemo, I had resigned myself to the fact that it was going to happen, like it or not. There was nothing else on the table.

In the meantime we had the unenviable task of organising radiation to my brain. We met with the radio oncologist that week and she offered me two different types of radiation, steriotactic radiation and full brain radiation. She explained she was running a clinical trial for the full brain version.

Steriotactic radiation is where the radiation is only applied to the site of the tumour, hopefully, I repeat hopefully, preventing any rogue cancer cells escaping to cause more brain tumours. Full brain radiation is when they apply radiation to the whole brain, which gives you a greater chance of killing any rogue cancer cells, but almost always leaves you a dribbling mess.

I don't think I have to tell you which radiation therapy we chose. Being a dribbling mess was not conducive with finding a way to save my own life.

I needed two appointments for this procedure, one to make a mask that perfectly moulded to my head and the other to receive the radiation waves. I heard how the mesh mask would be stapled down to a cradle on the bed so that my head would stay perfectly still. The appointments were two days apart.

The making of the mask wasn't pleasant at all, but the thought of wearing it and lying there while it covered my face and held me pinned to a cradle lifted me to another level of anxiety and fear. Poor Scott, I felt so sorry for him. He just had to try to comfort me, pep me up and console me day after day after day. It was a full-time job for him. I was so bloody lucky to have him there; he was rock solid. He never wavered.

Two days later we went back for the radiation. I knew this time I was going to have this claustrophobic mask over my head to receive the treatment. I can't fathom how those radiographers do their jobs every day, watching people scared, senseless and bewildered at where their life has taken them.

These people had the unenviable task of making smothering claustrophobic masks and administering radiation to people's organs. In my case it was to my brain. They truly deserve a medal. In fact they should be wearing one around their necks every single day.

Scott was with me when I walked into the room. I was almost hyperventilating at the thought of having to wear this tight mask, comparable to the one Jason Voorhes wore in the movie *Friday the 13th*. The mask would cover my whole head for twenty minutes while I was zapped with radiation. I was a nervous wreck.

I sat on the edge of the bed with my legs dangling and moving around like a little child who didn't want to lie back in the dentist's chair. 'You can do this,' everyone was encouraging me; Scott, the young guy who took me into the room, and the girl who was speaking through a microphone in a booth ready to zap me.

I had to do this. Brian the Brain Surgeon had said it was a 'must do', it would give me a better chance of keeping any more tumours at bay. No guarantees, of course, but a better chance all the same.

I tried to slow my breathing and calm myself down. *Mum, please talk to me, talk me through this*, I begged in my thoughts.

I finally lay down; they placed the mask over my head *and* stapled it to a plastic cradle on top of the bed. My breathing started to speed up once more and again I tried to slow it down, telling myself it would be over soon.

I had a buzzer to press if I became too distressed. Scott was stroking me. I had to get tough with myself. 'Okay,' I said to everyone, 'just do it.'

Scott squeezed my hand and said, 'I love you.' Then he had to leave the room.

I heard a click; he had taken a photo. *Why did he do that?* Who knows. I'm sure I've already told you he can be a bit strange sometimes.

That will be a nice photo for the grandkids. Grandkids. I was thinking about making it through this nightmare to see my future little grandchildren.

That was the best distraction I could have had. Instead of thinking about being under a mask that was nailed down so I could receive radiation to my brain, I just cried my way through the treatment wondering how I had got there. I couldn't move or sniff or make any noise, once again I just had to let the tears silently roll down my face.

Twenty minutes later it was over, I'd done it. They gave me the mask as a souvenir. Well that's what they said. I know it was in case I needed it again.

The same week I had to visit another radiologist to talk about radiation on my internal organs. I wasn't keen on the idea but I promised myself I would explore every option. The radiologist was nice, very knowledgeable and I quite liked her until she said, 'There's not much point in you having radiation at this stage' . . . then the clanger, 'I don't know how long you've got.'

Before I had the time to engage my filter, I blurted out, 'And I don't know how long you've got.' She glared at me like I was a crazy woman but I held her gaze. What the hell was the point in saying that? Was I not going through enough? Did she think I was an android with no feelings? All I could surmise was that she must have been away from university the day they taught 'Bedside Manner' along with quite a few of the other medicos, it seems.

Around that time our whole community knew what was going on, and a mountain of flowers, cards and meals appeared on our doorstep. Everyone was being so kind and caring. Up till that point I hadn't felt like seeing anyone other than my family, but I knew I couldn't hide in the dark forever. Still, I wasn't ready just yet. I had always been a confident, strong person and the thought of being pitied almost ate me from the inside out. I knew what everyone would be thinking and saying to each other. All of our friends knew about the brain tumour but, where possible, I kept the rest to myself. My mindset was that it was my body, my business.

Slowly, however, the determination and will to live, the will to get back to being me, a normal, fun-loving person, a mother, a wife, was manifesting deep inside of me. *We can do this*, I kept saying to myself. *We will find a way.*

And then, as soon as I would feel in a semi-good place and ready to conquer this thing, a monster would get in my head, right in the centre of my mind, and start sabotaging my thoughts. This wasn't me anymore; it was someone or something else.

Why do you think you can survive this when no one else does? he would say. Oddly, it was a male voice.

Because I can, I have to; I have kids who need me. You know that. A whole conversation going on in my head!

Yes, I know that, but who gets over stage four fast-moving advanced cancer?

I do. Now shut the fuck up.

This monster would taunt me on a regular basis so I ended up calling him the mean monster. It wasn't me, so I needed to have a clear definition of who was saying what in my head. It was crucial for my sanity, my survival.

He would say things like, *Look at that funeral car, will you be in there one day soon? Who do you think will do the eulogy? What song do you think they'll play?* He was hard to contain, he would show up when I was least expecting it and say the most horrible things.

Then there was another male voice, a soft, caring voice. He wanted to be my friend. He believed in me. He would say things like, *Look how well you are, you can do this. If anyone can do this you can.* He was a nice monster, just like the one in the kids' movie *Monsters Inc.*

One morning he popped up and gave me a song. He said, *Julie, sing this song whenever you think of it. It will help you focus, stay strong and put you in your future.* It went like this:

> *I am happy and healthy,*
> *All my organs have healed,*
> *My body and its organs have healed,*
> *I have faith in life.*

I felt like I had read that verse before, like it was buried somewhere in my subconscious. The nice monster has brought it back to my conscious mind. It was the perfect mantra and he knew I needed one, big time. So that was my song and I sang it with gusto. Just in my head when people were around, but out loud when no one could hear me. I loved him for giving me that song.

My first chemo treatment was looming and in between my radiation and other appointments I had a procedure to have a portacath implanted in my chest. It's a plastic device that can have a needle inserted in it for chemotherapy infusions, and works efficiently to get the drug into the bloodstream. It was an easier alternative to having a cannula inserted in my veins time and time again. I wasn't happy about having it there but then again I wasn't happy about much, and, quite frankly, it was the least of my worries.

I was booked in for my first infusion of chemotherapy in August 2012. It had now been seven weeks since my diagnosis and Scott and I were a little antsy about getting started on my treatment. To make matters worse I felt a lump on my back in the shower. I called out to Scott to come and look at it and I could tell by his expression that he already knew it was there.

I said, 'You knew, didn't you?'

'Yes,' he said softly. 'I didn't want to upset you.'

This may sound trivial compared with everything else I had going on but it was actually a big deal for me. It was the first time this 'thing' was a total reality. This thing that was apparently moving around inside of me had now become visible. It was a subcutaneous melanoma metastasis. I was inconsolable.

Then the day before I was due for treatment the hospital called, my kidney cancer drug, Pazopanib, had been ordered, but guess what? It got lost and nobody knew where it was. And no, I am not kidding.

I thought Scott was going to self-combust, he was so angry. He tried to call my usual oncologist but he was away at a conference. He was away a lot, actually, which became rather annoying. After ringing around for about half an hour, Scott finally located the company that had shipped the drug. They had no clue what had happened. By now Scott was losing it big time and to cut a very long story short, it took another frustrating week for the drug to arrive. So, that made it eight weeks from diagnosis to treatment with this unwelcome guest running amok in my body.

Chemo day finally arrived and I had mixed emotions. One part of me was relieved that I was at least doing something about my condition. The other part was devastated that I was going to hospital to have chemicals injected into my bloodstream. I was going to feel lethargic and nauseous, and my hair would fall out. Apparently I would be bald within a matter of weeks. That sucked.

The time came, we got in the car and headed south. It was a beautiful sunny winter's day but for my husband and me it was gloomy and grey. Even though I was in my bright colours, they had little effect on my mood.

I looked across at Scott as we drove over the bridge that crossed the lake near our home, one of my favourite places in the world, and he looked sad. I knew he would be hating the thought of me having chemotherapy – he didn't even like taking paracetamol. He would hate seeing me being infused with this poison that attacks the good cells as well as the bad, but he knew we had no choice.

As we passed the beach that day I saw him glance across to the ocean. He loves surfing, it's his passion; he calls it his religion, his church. I knew he wished he was out surfing those waves and it made me choke up to think I had done this to him. I wished he was out there surfing, too, so much that it hurt, but I needed him. Like all of us, this was something I thought I would never have to do. It would be torture without him by my side.

My girls knew what I was doing that day but I hadn't made a big deal of it. I asked Scott to do the same; the poor guy was torn between my wishes and what he thought the girls should know. Looking back, I probably did the wrong thing by keeping the seriousness of it from them, but I just wanted to protect them. I was the lioness and they were my cubs. I was going to get through this and they didn't need to worry. If I told them what might happen, they would question the promise I made to them and that would change everything. Scott was probably not so sure, although he has never said the words. He might have wanted to prepare them for the worst.

We arrived early that afternoon and went directly to the 'chemo room', but we had to have an initial consultation to prepare us for what lay ahead. The chemo nurse went through the details, most of which we already knew. She then said I would start losing my hair in about the third week of treatment. I was to be having chemo every week for, well, who knew how long, nobody could tell me the answer to that. They could only say that I would have a scan six weeks later to see whether I was responding.

She finished off our meeting by saying, 'We just need to keep you alive as long as we can and hopefully a clinical trial will come up that you are eligible for before it's too late.'

What the fuck!

Was she serious? Not the most comforting words I needed to hear in that moment. But she said them nonetheless. I guess it's her job to say stuff like that to people every day but it was my *life* she was talking about. I just stared at her. I'm pretty sure she knew I wasn't happy.

Now I don't know if you're aware of this or not, but there is such a thing as a 'chemo circle'. Yep, a gathering where everyone sits in a circle trying not to stare at each other while having a tube connected to their body delivering chemicals to their bloodstream intravenously because they have cancer.

The nurse led me over to a reclining chair, the last one available in the circle. There were three old ladies, two old men, and a woman about my age looking pale and sick with a scarf tied around her head.

I turned to Scott, looked him right in the eye, mouthed, 'I can't do this', and walked out of the room. He chased after me into the hall where I was crouched down on my haunches weeping uncontrollably. He picked me up, cuddled me and said, 'Sit down over here, I'll sort this out.'

The next minute, he and the nurse came over to me and led me to a small cubicle in the corner. She pulled the curtains around me and that was where I had my first chemotherapy infusion.

Chapter Nine

Two hours later it was over and we were on our way home. It was strange that I didn't feel the physical effects of the chemo drugs entering my system but the emotional effects were definitely there. I was tired; my mind couldn't take any more. I was on overload.

Was my body going to respond?

Was I going to be one of the 35 per cent?

I had to be, there was no other option!

If I didn't respond to this, I had none and Buckley's chance of responding to the ten and fifteen per cent options.

That afternoon, two of my sisters were travelling to the bush for a couple days to watch my niece play in a touch football tournament. I love touch football and have played for 30 years; I also really love watching it.

Scott had to go to a meeting so I was home on my own. Remy was at school and Morgan at work. I sat on the couch and just stared out the window.

Then I picked up my phone and called my baby sister, Nicole. The first thing she asked was, 'How are you feeling, Jule?'

'Okay,' I replied. 'Can I come to the country with you guys?'

'Of course,' she said, sounding a little surprised. 'We'd love you to come.'

I called Scott and told him I was going, but he was a little concerned as I was supposed to be resting and keeping away from people so I didn't pick up any bugs (because chemotherapy weakens the immune system). I've never been one to do what I am told, however, and I wasn't about to start. Finally we agreed it would be good for me to get away with my sisters and somehow get my mind off this bloody cancer for more than a minute at a time. I also wanted to show my girls this chemo thing was no big deal.

So I got up, threw some clothes into a bag and Nicole picked me up half an hour later. Definitely an impulse decision but I had to get away; I had to do something different.

I didn't mention it during that phone call with Scott, but I also wanted to give him a break from me and my unpredictable emotions. I was acutely aware of how draining it must have been for him. The day before, he was sitting at the desk he'd set up at home so he could look after me. I had something to say, something that had been insistently playing on my mind. I walked up behind him, put my hands on his shoulders and once again through tears I announced, 'If I don't make it through this, if I can't find a way out, you have to keep living your life and try to find a way to be happy. You have to tell the girls that I said the best gift they could give me would be to live the best lives they possibly can. I would never want to ruin their lives. Life is for living. I want them to keep loving me and always remember and talk about me but they have to be strong and keep living their lives.'

I could see his reflection on his computer screen, his eyes were closed. He had his arms crossed holding both of my hands on his shoulders.

'Please Scott, will you tell them? Do you promise?'

After a very long pause he responded, 'Yes, I promise,' knowing nothing else would appease me.

I added, 'I will do whatever it takes to find a way and between the two of us we can do anything.'

He tried to smile but we were both crying. If there was a crying event in the next Olympics we could cry for Australia and win gold!

The trip to the country was just what the doctor ordered. Well, Doctor Julie, that is. While I wasn't over the moon with the chemo, and I was feeling okay, I was a little comforted by the fact I was actually doing something about my situation. We talked and laughed and watched my niece play touch football. I love watching sport and it was one of the best distractions since this whole debacle had begun.

During one of the games I heard a beep on my phone, it was a text from Scott.

You are the most amazing person I know, I love you so much.
His words lifted my spirits even higher that day. I didn't think
that I was amazing, but I basked in the notion that he did.

Arriving back home from the trip, I felt a strange feeling
of peace. I knew it wouldn't last long but I was happy to
have it. I made an important commitment to myself that
day; I decided that I wouldn't call my condition a battle or
a fight. I just couldn't see the sense in fighting and battling
with my own body. From growing up in a family of five kids,
I knew that when you fight with something, guess what? It
fights back.

My T cells had become lazy and let cancer cells slip through.
It was my body, they were my cells, and I had to take responsibility for what had happened. So I decided to face my situation
head on.

That afternoon I changed into my exercise gear, called the
dog and we went out to the park directly behind our house.
Roxy was always so excited when I put on my trainers, she knew
she was going out the back to run amok chasing the rabbits
until she fell down with exhaustion. I felt like running that day,
so that's what I did. I ran for about fifteen minutes singing the
song the nice monster taught me. There was no one around so
I sang it out loud over and over again.

I am happy and healthy,
All my organs have healed,
My body and its organs have healed,
I have faith in life.

That song went everywhere with me, I sang it every time I thought about it. When my run was over I sat down on the log that bordered the garden where Roxy tirelessly chased the rabbits. Now it was time for me and my body to have a chat.

I closed my eyes and tried to picture all my organs and cells. *I'm sorry,* I said, *so sorry that I've let you down. I'm not exactly sure what it was, but it must have been something. Maybe you were trying to tell me something and I didn't listen. I take full responsibility for what has happened and I take responsibility to find a way back.*

It is what it is and now we have to work through it. I promise I will listen to you from now on. You say jump and I'll say, How high? *Together we can sort this out. I know we can. I have never thanked you before today for being the great body that you are and carrying me around for all these years, letting me dance and run and play sport. That was remiss of me and I'm sorry.*

I also thanked my cells and my organs. I asked them to work with me and restore my health. It wasn't strange for me to talk to myself; I'm a Gemini, after all, so there are two of us. I was always talking to myself but *never* on such a deep and emotional level. It was quite a revelation for me to have that chat and it felt rather extraordinary that I'd never done it before. I felt empowered, but I wasn't kidding myself that the road would be easy. I needed to be realistic about the whole thing. I had to. The mean monster didn't let me go too far into La La Land.

———

Around that time I had to have sixteen staples removed from my head. I'd been advised to take painkillers an hour before the procedure, so I did, and they were strong ones.

We hadn't seen the wound because it was concealed with lots of white medical tape. My dressing was removed and I was handed a mirror; I thought I'd be horrified but I actually felt quite the opposite. I was impressed with Brian's handiwork, it was a very neat wound, around twelve centimetres long with staples punched evenly throughout.

It went from right behind my left ear in line with my eyebrow down to the bottom of my earlobe in a dog-leg shape, and was well hidden from view. So, that was where my little uninvited visitor had been hiding. The little bugger that caused me to have my seizure in the office all those weeks ago. Weeks? It felt like years.

I will always be grateful that I was in the office that afternoon and not in my car. If it was three hours before or three hours after that life-changing moment, that's exactly where I would have been. It was only seconds from the time I felt strange to the seizure coming on at full speed. I would have almost certainly killed myself that day and most likely another poor unsuspecting motorist. If the seizure had to happen, then I'm thankful for the timing.

The staples all came out with ease, the painkillers worked and another job was done!

My second session of chemo came around earlier than welcomed. I still felt okay physically, but had to have my blood tested to make sure my white blood cell levels weren't too low.

My bloods were good so I could receive my next dose. I 'had' to be a big girl this time and join the chemo circle. Everyone else had to do it so why should it be any different for me? I just had to toughen up. This time there were only two others in the circle and quite a few empty chairs, so it wasn't as confronting. Although, one man in the circle, in his wisdom, was talking to a couple of student doctors, telling them at the top of his voice how chemotherapy had ravaged his body, describing all his health problems one by one.

I remember thinking how unprofessional it was of the hospital to allow this to happen. At that point I was just trying to stay alive, so a few ailments here and there wouldn't be such a big deal for me. But I did complain to the oncologist at my next visit as I felt strongly that I didn't want any other unsuspecting patient to have to sit and listen to that negative talk on top of everything else they were going through. He agreed to fix it.

I sent Scott home halfway through my second infusion. If this was going to be part of our new normal, I just had to suck it up and do it on my own. I didn't want him or anyone else sitting there with me in that environment, it only made me feel worse.

I wasn't allowed to drive for three months after the surgery as there was always the risk of having another seizure. That was frustrating; I missed my independence. My friend Liz, who has been my best friend since our first year of high school, offered to pick me up and I accepted. When I told her that I had a brain tumour on that fateful night her response had been, 'I can't breathe.' We had been close for such a long time.

When I walked out to meet her at the hospital gates, it was chilly and grey, but I felt okay. We chatted all the way home about anything but cancer. She came inside and we sat on my deck with the outdoor heater on, chatting for hours.

Liz got it; she didn't ask me the ins and outs of everything, she only talked about it if I brought it up. She knows me well and totally gets me. She was to become a huge part of my journey.

―――

After my third infusion of chemo I was standing in the shower washing my hair and felt a weird sensation between my fingers. I pulled my hands away and there it was.

My hair was coming out in clumps, great big handfuls. Yes, I was told it would happen but I thought for some ridiculous reason that maybe it wouldn't happen to me. You'd think I would have learned *that* lesson by now, but quite clearly I hadn't. I guess you could call it denial.

I took a step forward and banged my forehead gently on the glass of the shower recess. I was gutted, this was all too much. I rinsed off my hair and dried it very, very gently. I grabbed a towel, walked down the stairs, made a beeline for Scott and sobbed in his chest. I only found comfort in *his* arms. He didn't ask what had happened and I didn't want to say the words. He was expecting it, he just knew.

The following day I had my hair cut to my shoulders. I figured that if there was less weight in my hair I would have a better chance of keeping at least some of it. There I was, back in that little place called denial!

I was slowly venturing out in public a little more and trying to catch up with friends. I was told more than once that my new 'hairdo' bore a striking resemblance to Cameron Diaz, which was a lovely compliment but I know it was their way of making me feel better about losing my hair.

Some wellwishers said that losing my hair would be 'a small price to pay and not such a big deal'. What the hell does that mean? Losing your hair, your femininity, your identity was a *huge* price to pay. If I was knocking on heaven's door, I didn't want to be bald when someone opened it.

It made an already hideous situation almost unbearable. I was going to be as bald as a badger. My long blonde hair, my eyelashes and my eyebrows would soon disappear. Now call me shallow, but that, for me, was a big fucking deal. Another friend had told me it would feel great when the warmth washes over my nude skull in the shower.

She said it would be 'liberating'. Now I've looked up the meaning of 'liberating' and here it is: 'The feeling of freedom – being able to do what you choose without feeling restricted.'

So, since I was not experiencing any of these feelings in any way, shape or form, I politely suggested to her that she should shave her head and try it out for herself. I'm pretty sure that didn't happen.

Two comments I did find supportive at the time were, 'That sucks' from my sister and from a good buddy who said, 'Jesus, if you aren't going through enough already.'

Oh, and my friend Penny, who has short red hair, said, 'Don't worry, hair's overrated.' Now that was funny.

Most people think they have to say something, but I have learned from those experiences that it's okay to say nothing. My Nanna Sharkey used to say, 'If you don't know what to say to someone, say nothing and be careful how you say it.' She was a wise woman.

A quick non-patronising hug also works wonders. But hey, that's just me.

One Saturday a few weeks into the treatment, I had to come to terms with the fact that I needed a wig. The thought sickened me but it was my new reality. So my friend Trish offered to take me to a lady who had a showroom in her home full of wigs and hairpieces. Feeling nauseated, I tried on one wig after another. They looked weird on me and I was becoming more and more upset.

The worst part was that trying on the wigs was matting the little hair I had left. I was going out that night and was hoping for my last night of Cameron Diaz before I had to succumb to my fate. That didn't happen.

I went home, had a shower and tried to wash my hair. It was just a mass of thinning knots and looked like a very sparse bird's nest that would only house one tiny bird at best. It was over, I had to give in. I was devastated.

I'd bought a hairpiece that day as I wasn't coping with the wig thing. It was long blonde hair attached to four stretchy lace straps that you pulled over your head. You had to wear a cap or a scarf over it otherwise the bald bit would be poking through the top. Not such a good look. I got ready to go out and put the hairpiece over my matted clump that was still firmly stuck to my head and put a black baseball cap over the top. The synthetic hair was very long and it was obvious it wasn't mine.

I remember that afternoon so clearly. We were invited to our friends Fran and Pete's house for a barbecue with a few other couples. I was torn between not going at all and the fact that I needed to get out. We decided to go but I felt so awful all night. So lonely even in a room full of close friends. I was different from everyone sitting around the table. I felt like an alien, disconnected from the world. Scott said it wasn't obvious but I don't know how. I'm sure the women there could tell I was different. I wasn't me; I was much quieter than usual. The men might not have noticed. They don't usually pick up on stuff like that, god love them.

Monday came and the inevitable had to be done. I was finally allowed to drive so I got in the car with my hairpiece and black cap on, drove down the road and over the bridge to a local hairdressing salon. My hairdresser, Sarah, knew what was going on – she had given me the Cameron Diaz do. But I was just about to say goodbye to Cameron and say hello to Sinéad O'Connor, not someone I had willingly aspired to resemble.

I walked in; Sarah looked at me and motioned me towards a room at the back of the salon. I'd asked her for some privacy when I made the appointment. I sat in a chair with my head down. I heard the buzzing sound of the clippers and then she did it. She shaved off what was left of my hair. I didn't look in the mirror; I just put on my hairpiece and my black cap and I didn't feel liberated at all.

The weather was getting warmer, so I drove out to Newport Beach, a couple of kilometres from home, to a cute little boutique and bought myself a beautiful aqua full-piece swimming costume. I will never forget that day, that feeling and that cossie! I wanted to give my spirits a lift with something new. I wanted to dive into the ocean and swim out to the horizon. But instead I put my new blue cossie on, went to the beach, and waded in up to my waist as my synthetic hair wouldn't cope with the salt water.

That hairpiece was a lifesaver, well not literally, but it did become a very good friend to me. Apart from the people who knew me, no one seemed to notice that it wasn't my hair although it did look a little strange that I had a black baseball cap on at ten o'clock at night. I soon rectified that by introducing a black scarf.

I did end up buying a wig as I couldn't wear a cap when I renewed my driver's licence. I clearly remember that trip to the RTA. Scott suggested I should renew it for five years but without warning the mean monster had said, *Are you sure you're not wasting your money?*

I wore that wig to renew my passport and once to a lunch with my girlfriends. I felt like a freak, went home and threw it in the bin. It had cost $400 but I didn't care. On reflection I should have donated it to a cancer charity, but I wasn't thinking straight at the time. From then on it was the hairpiece with a black cap during the day and a black scarf at night. Not ideal but I had to make it work.

Chapter Ten

There are many horrible aspects of this condition and at the top of the list is the waiting.

Waiting for appointments, waiting for drugs, waiting for hair to fall out, waiting for answers and, the worst of all, waiting to find out if the chemotherapy I was putting into my system was actually having any effect.

Don't forget there was a big chance I was in the 65 per cent who didn't respond. But *I* had to be a responder, there was no option. I was desperate to have the scans; I needed to know the drugs were doing something. I wanted to create some hope, not just for me, but for my husband, my girls, my family and friends.

I had to wait another few weeks and that was excruciating. Part of me was scared senseless that the treatment wasn't working and I would be one step closer to a fate I couldn't contemplate.

After my deep and meaningful chat with my body's cells and organs I had to start moving forward with a plan. I had to broaden my horizons. I had to stop focusing on chemo and find a way to give my body the best chance of coming through it with the least possible damage to my health, mentally *and* physically. There would be more to do, I just knew it.

My sister Nicole had heard about a girl who had thyroid cancer ten years prior and swore by the teachings and lifestyle of a guy called Bill Giles who was a medical biologist who offers a support program for cancer patients. Bill works with the immune system and uses a holistic approach to balance the mind and body and had worked with many patients over the years with a personalised approach to their illness. This was a combination of diet, herbs, self-awareness and spiritual practice. I needed to stay well and alert, that was a given. So I called and made an appointment to chat with Bill over the phone.

Bill is a nice enough guy but he didn't beat around the bush with his response when I told him about my condition. 'Julie,' he said, 'on a scale of one to ten, melanoma cells are a nine in terms of their power to reproduce and make more tumours and it sounds like they have had a field day in your body. But come and see me, I will teach you how to give yourself the best possible chance of staying well for as long as possible.'

Bill was in Canberra, around four hours from home, where all the politicians rant and rave, act like two-year-olds and make promises they don't keep. I was hoping this wasn't going to be the case with Bill. I needed to do this; I needed to get my head in the game. I made an appointment for the following week and thanked my body for giving me that message, for telling me to look outside the box.

I know I keep banging on about this, but I hated being bald. I wasn't one of those brave women who just walked around loud and proud with no hair. I admired them but I just wasn't one of them. I always had a scarf on my head as a bare minimum.

Scott didn't say or do anything to make me feel different or less sexy, although I'm guessing he regretted a comment he'd made years before when we were dating. Swanning around on a beautiful island on the Great Barrier Reef, I had dived into the pool and was daintily breaststroking towards him; he was standing in the pool staring at me with a bemused look on his face. I stood up and looked him in the eyes; I was so in love. I actually thought this could be it, a marriage proposal. But I couldn't have been any further off the mark. He put his arms around me and made a request.

'Do me a favour, darl,' he said, 'never go bald.'

Quite clearly my long blonde hair was not a good look when it was wet and plastered to my head and he felt compelled to let me know. This thoughtless comment had now come back to bite him on the arse.

But I will say in his defence that he did refrain from changing the words of the Bee Gees song 'More Than a Woman' to 'Bald-headed Woman', which were his preferred lyrics before this whole cancer thing began. When the song played on the radio in the car he just shut up or changed the station. I had to be thankful for that. I do have a good sense of humour but I don't think even I would have found that funny.

I didn't look forward to much in those days but I was looking forward to our meeting with Bill the Biologist because I wanted to gather as many tools as I could to keep my body functioning in the most efficient way possible. It was worth the long drive. While his words were all very scientific, we managed to grasp some of the concepts. He understood the body at a cellular level and explained what effects certain foods and lifestyle choices had on the immune system. He advised me to cut sugar, gluten and grains out of my diet and gave me a strict program to follow. He also gave me some herbal potions to support my organs and strict instructions that meditation and yoga were essential. He recommended that I make a collage of my future and my dreams and put it on a wall where I could look at it every day.

He finished off by saying, 'You need to experience joy and laughter. You have to be joyful as much as you can then your cells will respond to your joy.'

I appreciated the tip, and would give this my best shot, but being joyful all the time under my current circumstances would be easier said than done.

Scott and I left Bill's office feeling a little better than before. We booked into a hotel that night and decided to go out, have a nice meal and share a bottle of red wine. I thought I'd get right onto the 'experiencing joy' part of Bill's plan. This was my last hurrah as wine was now a no-no in my new diet.

I enjoyed every drop of my cabernet sauvignon that night and the lovely meal Scott and I shared. Little by little I kept building my resolve to be well again, to be free from disease, but I wasn't spared a visit from the mean monster.

Do you really think that going on a special diet will save you? Really Julie, you're an intelligent woman and you're going to buy into that? He was relentless.

I actually told him to piss off.

Then the nice monster comforted me and told me not to listen to him. *Just sing your song and do what Bill said. You are strong, you can do this.*

I went home and made my collage. I used pictures of hot women with long hair, stunning holiday locations, beautiful clothes, surfboards and a little child playing sport, representing my future grandchild. I pasted on a picture of the Queen and to this day I don't know why. Delusions of grandeur? Or maybe I wanted her to send me a card when I turned 100. That would mean she would have to live another 50 years, which may have been stretching it a bit.

I also put up a picture of a watch to represent time. This might seem strange, but it was reflecting the notion that it was up to me. I could have much more time on this earth if I stayed strong in mind, body and spirit. I also put the figure 2048, which was the year I wanted to live beyond. My collage was on a purple piece of cardboard, my favourite colour. I loved it and took it everywhere I went. If I left home for more than one night, I stared at it constantly so the images and the words were burned into my brain.

I had never been particularly spiritual, nor had I done any yoga or meditation. I'd always viewed these as a waste of time when I could be running, going to the gym or playing touch football. Things needed to change, though, so I gobbled up all the information I could on anything that would comfort me, help me grow spiritually, nurture my body and keep me strong.

How lucky are we to have the internet? I believe the world wide web helped save my life. After learning all I could about yoga, I decided to team up with a personal yoga instructor – I needed the one-on-one connection. I teamed up with Stephanie, who was a godsend. Doing yoga with her twice a week truly played a huge part in keeping me strong and maintaining my sanity. Could we afford it? No, but money wasn't high on the priority list at the time.

Stephanie would come around and do yoga with me and Roxy. We would go outside on my back deck overlooking the park and I would get lost in the postures and my breathing while trying very hard to stay in the moment. I would silently practise gratitude and be grateful for my life, my family and my friends. Doing yoga in nature was my favourite part of the week. It unexpectedly gave me a strong sense of the enormity of the universe and what a minute part I played in existence. Paradoxically, it also gave me the feeling that we are everything. Everything and nothing, all at once. I was surprised at how spiritual I was becoming. I didn't go around preaching this, but on the inside I was occasionally experiencing peace and these tiny pockets of peace were crucial in helping me survive.

We would finish off our sessions with a meditation and Roxy would snuggle up next to me while Stephanie patted her to stop her from barking for attention. Roxy used to be even more excited than me when Stephanie knocked on the door. Bill was right; yoga was to become an essential part of my healing.

My new diet wasn't easy but I stuck to it. I was determined. No bread, no pasta, no beer, no wine, ouch! Although Bill did say I could have a couple of brandies or tequilas, which was a relief. Sometimes it had to be done at the end of the day just to stop my mind and the monsters from taking over.

I gained a third monster. He was, well, 'sensible' is probably the best word for him. He wasn't mean and he wasn't overly friendly either. In fact he was very pragmatic. He would tell me that everything I was doing was great but it wasn't going to save me long term. He would tell me not to get swept away with all my newfound spirituality and to be realistic about my situation. He would tell me that there's a big world out there and that I needed to open my eyes. I wasn't really sure what he meant, but I would find out soon enough.

Six weeks into my treatment it was D-Day. It was time for the positron emission tomography (PET) scan, which would measure the amount of metabolic activity I had in my body. In other words, how much glucose the tumours were taking up, as this is how they divide and conquer. I'd had a PET scan before I started my treatment as a marker for the tumours before and after. This scan would tell the tale of whether the melanoma was on the rise or on the decline. It *had* to be the latter.

We had an early appointment at the western Sydney hospital. I couldn't have anything to eat or drink before the scan, so by the time we arrived I was hungry, thirsty, cranky and scared. This was it. The scan would tell me if my body was responding to the chemo. Scott had to wait outside. I'd taken anti-anxiety medication that morning as my stress levels were through the roof. When it kicked in I felt a little calmer, but I was acutely aware that by the end of this day I would know my fate.

If it wasn't working, what would I do? It would mean my tumours were aggressive and therefore it was highly likely, if not a certainty, that they would not respond to any other treatment.

The doctor injected me with fluorescent dye, wrapped me in a blanket and told me to have a lovely sleep for half an hour while we waited for the dye to spread around my body, then he could run the scan.

'Yes, I'm sure I will,' I said to him sarcastically as he left me alone.

That was a very long half hour. Luckily the PET scanning machines were not too overbearing so I could keep my claustrophobia in check.

The scan took about fifteen minutes and then it was over. It's so frustrating to know these people can see everything inside your body. But they can't tell you, they're not allowed to give you the slightest bit of a hint, even if it's good news. More waiting!

One of the doctors led me through the pre-exit lounge and gave me a plastic container of mixed triangle sandwiches and a little bottle of orange juice, all of which I couldn't consume as they were definitely not on my new diet.

This day has to get better, surely, I whispered to myself.

We knew we would find out the results that day, my oncologist had promised us. He said if we took the first appointment in the morning he would ring through and get the results that afternoon. I had endured quite a few 'longest days of my life' during this ordeal, but this day was definitely right up there with the worst.

I had many conflicting emotions going on in my head. It wasn't the monsters talking; there was no room for them that day. It was just me. My mind was jumping from one outcome to the other. I needed some good news. I knew it wouldn't be my long-term answer but it would just give me a break for a while, a bit of space. I wanted to be able to tell my family that my body was willing to respond. It was so important to me. And then the other thoughts came, just like a game of table tennis in my head. What if I hadn't responded? What if things had got worse? What if I had more tumours, bigger tumours? What if I was going to die soon? Had I been a good enough person? Had I loved my husband and children enough? Had I been a bitch too often? Had I given enough to the world? I knew that was a 'no'! Had I done all the things I always said I would do? Another 'no'. How would Morgan and Remy cope without me? Would Scott hook up with some young floozy? That thought was too much to bear.

We fluffed about on the way home, stopping for food, petrol, even though we didn't need any, stopping for coffee, even though I didn't drink it. Without saying it, we both knew what was coming and were trying unsuccessfully to distract ourselves.

We finally arrived home. I was feeling sick, devastated that I had to live like this. I took Roxy out to the park but not for long, I had to get back to Scott. I wouldn't take the call without him by my side.

It was 3.15pm when my mobile phone rang very loudly. I didn't want to miss the call so I'd turned up the volume. I looked down at my phone and there it was, my oncologist's name was flashing on my screen. My heart dropped to the floor and a huge lump suddenly appeared in my throat. I felt sick.

I couldn't cope, I handed the phone to Scott. We were in our bedroom; he sat on the bed and answered the phone.

'Hi Doctor, it's Scott.' Then he proceeded to say, 'Okay, okay, okay,' and then, 'I'll put her on.'

I reluctantly took the phone, and he said down the line, 'I have the results of your PET scan and I have great news: you are responding to the chemo, your tumours are shrinking and some have even disappeared.' In that second I became euphoric.

He went on to say, 'The radiologist actually asked me, "What is this girl doing?"'

I looked at Scott and handed him the phone. I couldn't speak. I slid down the wall of our bedroom, put my hands on my face and howled like a wolf. Scott finished the call, and slid down next to me, tears streaming.

I had responded!

We had time to breathe. We had some hope. I was in the 35 per cent, that group I so desperately wanted to join. I went back out into the park with Roxy, singing my song and thanking my body over and over again. I was elated.

On my way back home the sensible monster made a brief appearance. *Remember what I told you?* he said. *Keep your eyes open Julie, this journey is far from over.*

Chapter Eleven

Rock solid as always, my family arrived one by one to celebrate the good news. This time my brother was armed with a very big bottle of French champagne.

Champagne definitely wasn't on my new 'Bill' diet but I snuck in a glass anyway. I told myself it would have been rude not to. We were all relaxed, laughing and joking, happy like before.

They'd all known I was having that crucial scan. They would've been beside themselves. I had been in their position more than once and it was horrible, draining, all-consuming and terrifying. You couldn't concentrate on anything else. If something awful was happening to one of us, it was happening to all of us. I loved being able to give them good news that afternoon; it was a huge relief.

I have the best family in the world. For that I will be eternally grateful. Morgan and Remy were over the moon when we told them the news. Although I certainly didn't let on how crucial the scan results actually were. I hadn't thought far enough ahead; I didn't know what I would have said to them if the results weren't good. I couldn't fathom it so I didn't let my mind go there. Thank god I didn't have to have that conversation with them.

September arrived and so did Morgan's twentieth birthday. My beautiful big girl was turning twenty and wanted to celebrate with a party at home. I had begun to lose my eyebrows and eyelashes along with my hair. Saying I didn't feel very attractive is an understatement and I certainly didn't feel like entertaining. But that was just too bad. I had to suck it up and get on with it. It was Morgan's birthday and she wanted her mum there at the party doing mum things.

I did my best not to look too much like a sick person. Make-up became my best friend, although I have never been particularly good at applying it. The eyebrows I drew on made me look very similar to Bozo the Clown but hey, at least I had some. There wasn't much I could do about the eyelashes. I did think about the stick-on ones from the pharmacy but decided that would just be going a little too far.

After all it was Morgan's birthday that day, not mine. Then out of the blue when I was least expecting it, the mean monster caught me off-guard.

Do you think you'll be here to see Morgan turn 21? he asked rather casually.

I got rid of him immediately but I would be lying if I said his question didn't rock me to the core. How could he say that to me when I'd just received such good news? Not being alive for my daughter's 21st, really? Come on, that just couldn't happen. I wouldn't let it happen.

I actually managed to have fun with Morgan and her friends just like back in the good old days. All the girls looked gorgeous in their tight little mini dresses and sky-high shoes and the boys looked handsome. I hadn't seen many of her friends for a while, basically since all hell had broken loose a few months earlier.

It was an emotional experience cuddling them one by one as they walked into our home. They didn't say anything. They didn't have to, the hugs were saying it all. It was great to sit back and watch them laughing, dancing and singing along to the music. Twenty, wow, my little Morgie wasn't a teenager anymore!

She really is a remarkable girl, extremely talented in so many ways. She's an amazing dancer, and teacher. She plays guitar and sings, she's bubbly and bright but what makes Scott and I so proud is that she is a wonderful, caring person and now she was becoming a grown-up, a beautiful young woman. She does swear a tad too much. I have no idea where she got that from!

What a shame she had to deal with this horrible situation at such a young age – nothing remotely like this had happened to me when I was young. The first real sadness I had to deal with was when my Pa, my dad's dad, died suddenly of a heart attack when he was 80. I was 22 at the time. It was terrible, of course, but not a total shock. Morgan and Remy had lost their grandmother eleven years before, watched their auntie whom they adored go through breast cancer twice, and now me. It made me angry that they had to endure all of this sadness when they should be swanning around without a care in the world.

And the worst part of all, though, was that there was absolutely nothing Scott or I could do about it except hope that somehow, in some way, this horrible event would make them stronger women, and teach them not to take life for granted, to reach for the stars and be crystal clear in that being on this earth is a privilege, not a right.

I was so grateful to be a part of the birthday celebrations that night, regardless of how I looked, but it turns out my husband, Scott, was more into his looks than ever.

I've made it pretty clear so far that Scott can be a little, well, let's just say, different. Adorable, but different and even through that very dark period of our life there was no exception. One spring day I was sitting on the couch looking at him across the room, when I noticed that his hair had grown longer and he was growing a beard. After staring for some time to make sure I wasn't hallucinating, I asked him, 'Are you growing your hair *and* a beard?'

He looked across at me unperturbed and said, 'Yeah, do you think I look like Brad Pitt?'

Well, can you imagine? I didn't know whether to laugh or cry. There I was with no hair, no eyebrows and no eyelashes, going through the most scary, uncertain time of my life and he was going out of his way to resemble Brad Pitt!

Correct me if I'm wrong, but normal husbands would have gone out in sympathy and shaved their heads to support their partners, but not him. He took the opposite approach, god love him. To this day he is running with that so-called Brad Pitt look. I don't think he realises that Brad has had an update.

I guess we all cope with a crisis in different ways. Actually, he looks more like Jesus to me, and maybe that's who he was actually trying to be. Scott was hoping he could perform a miracle.

Sleeping did not come easily in those days and I didn't need anything else to rock the boat. One particular night in between chemo infusions I woke up around 3am in a pool of sweat. It was running from every one of my pores as though someone had turned a tap on in my head. It wasn't a hot night. I looked over at Brad Pitt and he still had the covers firmly snuggled up to his neck.

I got up, went to the bathroom and looked in the mirror. My face looked like it was on fire. I sat on the edge of the bath and ripped the scarf off my head. *What the hell was going on?*

The sweat from my face was dripping onto the floor. We didn't even have the fans out of storage yet. It was only September! All I could do was go downstairs and out onto the back deck, sit on a stool and hope to cool down. It didn't work. Then it kept happening night after night.

My next chemo was scheduled that week along with a visit to the oncologist. He was very happy about my great results and proud of himself for prescribing the combination drugs that had yielded such good results. He reiterated that even the radiographers were excited about the massive improvement. I joked with him that he would soon be featuring on the next edition of '*Oncology Weekly*', which made his chest puff out just a little more. There's no such magazine but I could tell he really loved the idea of it.

As far as I know I was the first person in Australia to trial this combination therapy and no doubt he was excited to have another weapon in his arsenal to offer future patients in the same, unenviable position. And, honestly, I was really happy about that too. Being in this big scary world of cancer gives you an intrinsic empathy for anyone who has walked this path before you and any poor unsuspecting person who will do so in the future.

He eventually asked me how I was feeling and if I had any questions. 'Actually, yes,' I said, 'I do feel good but I have a question. Why would I be sweating like a pig all the time, but profusely in the middle of the night? Would this be a side effect of the treatment?'

'Oh yes,' he said, 'didn't I tell you the Abraxane [the breast cancer drug] will have put you into menopause?'

'Oh fabulous,' I said in my usual sarcastic tone, followed by, 'and *no*, you didn't tell me.'

Just what I needed, going into menopause and dealing with all of those issues while trying to cope with everything else. They were not fun times.

Scott got the fans out of storage and I just had to cope the best way I could. Obviously I was 50, there was no denying that. I certainly didn't want any more children. But the timing was just a little out. I hadn't even noticed skipping a period.

Trying to find the positives as always, I managed to come up with a couple. No more periods, now that was a good thing, and I also figured it would save me a few bucks at the chemist.

After having chemo once a week regularly for the previous eight weeks, I had started to feel numbness in my fingers and toes. Unlike the menopause, I had been warned that this would probably happen. It was a weird sensation and it meant that my nerves were being damaged by the chemicals.

You might think that's nothing, and well, just deal with it, but I didn't like it, not one bit. Apart from the menopause, which was the pits, I was actually coping really well with the chemo. I didn't feel nauseous or sick at all. I'd managed to keep up my yoga and continued walking and running *and* singing my song every chance that I had.

I am happy and healthy,
All my organs have healed,
My body and its organs have healed,
I have faith in life.

My girls' birthdays are fairly close together, so now it was Remy's turn to have a gathering. She was turning seventeen. This time I was prepared. I didn't get all precious about my looks; I just frocked up and got on with it. I love all her friends. Just like Morgan's, they are full of beans and are a welcome reminder of what life's all about. They all looked divine and had so much fun laughing and singing and carrying on like silly buggers. Remy is a special young woman. She is quietly sensitive and funny, which is very endearing. And like her big sister, she's talented in so many ways. She was staying close to me like never before – she was scared and I knew it. She is gorgeous and caring. Scott and I are just so proud of her. What lucky parents we are; we must have done something right.

As the days went on, I found the nerve tingling and discomfort more and more distressing, so I decided to change my chemo infusions to fortnightly instead of weekly. Why? Well, I was following my gut.

I knew the numbness was from too many chemicals going into my bloodstream at short intervals. If my nerves were being affected, then what else was being damaged? I just knew I had to keep my body functioning at full capacity. I also reasoned that if I stretched out my infusions it would take longer for the cancer cells to build up a resistance, causing the drugs to stop working.

It was just a strong feeling I had. I was resolute about staying in my own lane and going with my instincts. This might not work for everyone, but for me, it's just what I had to do.

I explained this to my oncologist at my next visit. He didn't really understand my logic but surprisingly, given that he's the doctor and I'm the patient, he went along with my plan. He knew I was as stubborn as a mule.

It was late October and there was another burning question I had been wanting to ask him for a while. It was one of the hardest questions I've ever had to ask and the truth is I really didn't want to know the answer. But it was a question I *had* to ask for my very survival. There was no easy way to ask so I just blurted it out. 'How long will this treatment work for me?'

'Put it this way,' he said matter-of-factly, 'it won't be working in March.'

I felt sick and dizzy and all those morbid feelings came bubbling to the surface again. He was saying that the cancer was coming back in under five months and we all knew there was nothing else on the table. We were devastated.

We had known this treatment wasn't the answer long term. We had been told that my condition was a death sentence, the words 'life expectancy' were said more than once. Chemo was only a stopgap, not a cure, but we had hoped we had more time than that. I stared down at the checked linoleum floor in his office for a couple of minutes, then pulled myself together and found some of my inner warrior. 'Well, if you think we're going to hang around and wait for that to happen, you have another thing coming,' I announced.

By then my voice was shaking. Scott asked him if there was anything else, any treatment or trials anywhere in the world experimenting with drugs for melanoma. He told us there were a few clinical trials overseas that he would email us some information about but they all had around a 38 per cent response rate and they don't really like to take overseas patients as it makes things complicated *and* they cost a fortune.

How can you put a price on someone's life? I thought incredulously. Scott and I had already decided that we would live in a tent if that's what it took to keep me alive and keep our precious little family together.

'Is there any chance you can get us in to one of these clinical trials overseas, please?' I asked with a hint of desperation.

'No,' he said. 'I'm sorry. If you go down that path you will have to do it yourselves. I can send a referral if you find a suitable trial, but it won't be easy.'

We were speechless; we couldn't believe what we were hearing. We were now on our own; we would have to find a way to keep me alive all by ourselves. We felt abandoned by our country's medical system. I had often felt alone since my diagnosis, but that news took my loneliness to a whole new level.

Chapter Twelve

On our way home, after a long period of uncomfortable silence, I started barking out orders. 'I am going to find another treatment and you are going to have to help me do it. I'm not hanging around, waiting until March for the chemo to stop working and have the cancer take over. I'm doing everything I can to keep my body and my mind the healthiest they can be but I am not silly enough to think I can do this on my own. There's something out there that can help me and we are going to find it. I don't want to die.'

'Okay,' Scott said. 'Yes we will.'

'Don't just say, "Yes we will", say, "I promise we will."'

'I promise,' he said, sounding a little jaded.

The second I walked into our house I brushed past Roxy, much to her disgust, and headed straight for the computer.

I googled and I googled until I couldn't google any more. It was an absolute minefield. There were many clinical trials and experimental drugs and treatments all around the world. But there was one type of therapy that stood out from the rest. It was called immunotherapy, working with an experimental drug called PD-1, which stands for 'programmed cell death 1'.

I am going to get a little scientific here because I want to give you the full picture of what this treatment is about and why I became obsessed with it.

PD-1 is a protein that in humans is encoded by the PDCD1 gene. It's a cell surface receptor that belongs to the immuno-globulin super family. This protein is expressed on T cells and pro B cells and if successful, results in the activation of T cells and cell-mediated immune responses against tumour cells or pathogens. Activated PD-1 negatively regulates T cell activation and plays a key role in tumour evasion. In other words this scientific chain of events revs up the immune system so it can do its job. That job is to seek and destroy the tumour cells.

The PD-1 trial, working specifically with advanced melanoma patients, was being carried out in the US and in Spain. I called Scott over to my computer and we sat down and read as much as we could about the drug, the trials and the results they were achieving.

The next day we swung into action. The trial in the US appealed to us the most as we preferred not to have to deal with the language barriers in Spain along with everything else.

We worked out the time difference, looked up the tele-phone number of the hospital where the clinical trial was being conducted and nervously made the call. The name of the nurse running the clinical trial was Daniel Jackson. Disappointingly, the call went through to an answering machine.

'Hi Daniel,' I said with every muscle in my body twitching, 'my name is Julie Randall and I am from Australia.' By now my voice was quavering. 'I have stage four advanced metastatic melanoma and apart from chemotherapy that apparently will not be working in a few months' time, there is nothing here in Australia to help me. My husband and I are very interested in the clinical trial using the drug PD-1. We have two beautiful daughters who need their mother and we will do whatever it takes for me to stay alive for as long as I can.' By then I was sobbing.

I somehow pulled it together enough to leave our contact numbers and asked if he would call us back any time, day or night. I also left our email addresses. I hung up the phone and collapsed in a heap.

This situation was surreal. I had called a hospital in America on the other side of the world in a place called Portland, Oregon, wherever the hell that was. I was pleading for a place in a stage one clinical trial to give me some sort of chance of staying alive. Actually, it was beyond surreal.

At around that time our friends and family held a fundraiser for us at one of our local surf clubs. I absolutely hated the fact that this had to be done, but I was overwhelmingly grateful that we had such amazing and devoted family and friends. I had requested that no one talk to me about it as it was just too much for me to bear. I've always been a very proud person and the thought of people having to put their hands in their pockets for us just ate away at me.

But I had to acknowledge that we were already suffering financially and we were only four months in. We will be eternally grateful for what each and every one of those generous, wonderful people did for us in our quest to keep me alive.

I couldn't attend the evening, it was just too overwhelming. So, Scott and I went into the city and tried to occupy ourselves with restaurants and bars and people watching. But five minutes wouldn't pass without us thinking about how so many people were gathering together to help our family. I later found out that there were more than 500 people at the event – *wow*!

How do you personally thank 500 people? We felt honoured that so many people cared about us. I hope they all read this book and know how much Scott and I appreciated their kindness.

Once the event was over I couldn't think of anything else besides hearing back from Portland about their clinical trial. I became obsessed. The concept of the body helping itself to heal was a revelation to me. To give it a little help to kick the immune system back into action to identify the cancer cells and start destroying them with the ultimate goal of bringing the body back into harmony – it just made sense at a time when nothing else did.

This treatment still only had roughly a 38 per cent response rate, but it wasn't chemotherapy and it only attacked the cancer cells, not the healthy ones. There were some associated side effects but most of them were not severe and if they happened to me, well, I could deal with them if it meant I would be with my family for as long as I possibly could. It gave us hope.

Forty-eight hours went by without any contact from the clinical nurse. So, I called again and left another message. Scott also got on the job and found an email address for the clinical trials department and shot off an email.

Finally, one November morning we were at home; I was downstairs doing the washing and Scott was at his desk when the house phone rang. I heard it and ran upstairs just as Scott picked it up. He got straight up off his chair and walked out onto the deck.

I knew who it was just by his demeanour and then he finally said in a very Aussie way, 'Thanks mate for calling us back.'

It was him, Daniel Jackson, the nurse who headed up the PD-1 clinical trial in Portland.

My heart took its usual position in my throat. Then Scott said, 'I'll just put her on.'

'Hello,' I said, choked up as usual.

'Hi Julie, how are you?' he asked in a welcoming American accent.

Well that was it. I handed the phone back to Scott, who put him on speaker while I tried to pull myself together enough to explain the gory details of my condition.

Daniel was positive about the trial but did confirm the fact that only a third of patients responded. He went on to say most of those who had responded were doing well. The study was only in stage one, and there would be three stages to the full clinical study, so it was still early days to predict the long-term future for patients. By then I had pulled myself together and apologised to Daniel for losing the plot. He was very understanding.

Then I just blurted out the question, 'How do we get into this trial, Daniel?'

'Well,' he said, 'this is a very unusual situation; we have never had anyone applying from Australia before, so I will have to talk to the study team when we meet tomorrow and see what I can find out for you. I have your email address, Scott, so I will get back to you as soon as I can.'

'Thanks Daniel!' we said in unison.

Scott hung up the phone, we looked at each other with wry smiles and had a cuddle. Once again we had hope. Hope is such a powerful emotion but we also didn't want to build those hopes up too high. We had done that before and had them crushed in a monumental way.

Of course we'd wanted to know immediately if I could take part in the trial. We would have gotten on a plane the next day if they gave us the green light. But yet again we had to play the waiting game.

A few nights later Scott, the girls and I had a barbecue out on our back deck. It was a gorgeous balmy night – summer was definitely on its way. We were all out there with Roxy at our feet having a lovely time.

I didn't tell our girls about our recent phone call with America; there was no point throwing them into disarray until we had more information. But my mind couldn't stop trying to work out how we would manage the logistics of such a mammoth move if we were given the green light. The duration of the study was two years. I couldn't possibly go on my own. Not to begin with, anyway. I would want everyone to come but that wouldn't be possible.

Morgan was a dance teacher, it was her career; she was twenty years old and couldn't just up and leave her job. Remy was about to do her Higher School Certificate, her final year at school. How could she just drop everything and come to the US? I wanted so much for her to graduate – I couldn't bear the thought that this whole cancer thing would stop her from finishing school.

Scott had his business, our livelihood.

The mean monster didn't help matters, either. *How the hell do you think you can afford to live overseas for two years?* he asked rudely. *You can't leave your children behind. What if you only have twelve months to live – or less? Do you want to spend it away from your babies?*

I told him to shut his trap and that we needed to find a long-term fix for my girls, and that there would be *no* months-to-live scenario, thank you very much, and to get the hell out of my head.

I had to force myself to jump back into the present moment and enjoy our time together that night. I love my little family more than anything in the world.

The girls excused themselves and went about their business – texting, liking, Snapchatting or whatever they did to amuse themselves while Scott and I finished off our meals. Then, for some reason, I looked down at my phone and saw the date, it was 9 November 2012. It was our 21st wedding anniversary and neither of us had twigged. Our marriage is sacrosanct and we had always treated our anniversary as a special day, so the fact we had both missed it was heartbreaking.

I put my hand on Scott's leg and said, 'Guess what day it is?'

He thought for a few seconds and then he just looked at me and said a word that rhymes with truck!

With everything that was going on we could both be forgiven for not knowing what day it was, literally. Let alone a significant event. For me, though, it was devastating as I kept being reminded that I might not make the next one.

I wanted another 30 anniversaries. I wanted to live until I was well into my 80s and hopefully beyond. After all, it was on my vision board, the one that Bill the Biologist had encouraged me to create.

My husband is the man I love with all my heart. I have never called him my best friend. I have sisters and girlfriends for that. I know a lot of people do call their partners their best friends, but I have never felt that way. I don't want to have sex with my best friend, nor do I want to have a mortgage or share bank accounts or sleep in the same bed as them. I don't want to raise children with my best friend or wash their smelly underwear or worry about their odd socks. And if I had half as many arguments with my best friend they certainly wouldn't be my best friend anymore.

Scott is so much more than my best friend. He is my lover, my confidant, my sparring partner, my boxing bag; he is my favourite man in the world, warts and all. Though we don't share blood he is very much my family. We share a home; we share our children. He is my soulmate. I think you'll agree that he has earned that title.

We would take a bullet for each other and just for the record I wouldn't want my best friend telling me how to drive, how to hang washing on the line correctly or showing me the best way to boil an egg.

Yes, best friends are very special but very different in my eyes.

In the end, Scott and I didn't worry too much about missing our anniversary that year. We had bigger fish to fry!

———

Another 24 hours had passed and we hadn't heard back from the US, so I fired off an email to Daniel Jackson.

> Hi Daniel,
>
> It's Julie Randall here. Thanks again for calling us back yesterday. We were just wondering if you've had a chance to talk to the team about our participation in the clinical trial.
>
> Daniel, I have two young daughters, they need their mother. I am fit and healthy and I am sure I will cope with the treatment.
>
> Looking forward to hearing back from you asap.
>
> Warm regards,
> Julie Randall and family

I even had a chuckle to myself when I typed that email, begging my way into a clinical trial to try to save my life while spouting on about how fit and healthy I was. It was laughable, but in my mind I *was* fit and healthy. There was nothing wrong with me. Nothing on the outside, anyway. Even the lump on my back had disappeared.

It was about eight hours later when I sat down to check my emails. I pressed the send/receive button and there it was, the name I wanted to see right there on the left of the very first message in my inbox – Daniel Jackson.

Hi Julie,

Yes I did speak to the team yesterday and they think there would be a lot of red tape and complications for you to take part in the clinical trial here in Portland.

The fact that we have totally different health cover and you would not be covered under our system if you were to have any complications from the treatment.

I will forward you some information about clinical trials and other drugs that are being tested in Australia. Sorry we couldn't help you. Good luck.

Kind regards,
Daniel Jackson

For about two minutes I was gutted, we were gutted. I read it out to Scott and then my determination kicked back in. I had to compose myself.

I was going to get into this clinical trial in Portland, Oregon, no matter what. So I didn't hesitate, I just banged out another email right away.

Hi Daniel,

Thank you for your response, but I'm sorry, I can't accept your team's decision based on the reasons that you explained. As I said previously, apart from the melanoma, I am very fit and healthy. I'm walking and sometimes running on a daily basis. My blood results will prove this and I will forward them to you straight away.

As for the financial side of it, if you can work out a figure that you and your team are comfortable with that would cover me for any perceived complications, then we would be happy to transfer the money at your request.

Thank goodness my husband isn't putting a price on my life and we will do whatever it takes to be in the trial.

Thank you for sending me information about trials and drugs in Australia, I really appreciate your help, however there has been no stone unturned in that department.

I do not qualify for any clinical trials here and have researched all of the drugs available and none of them are suitable for me.

If you could please go back to your team and address the perceived issues with our proposed solutions, that would be much appreciated. Oh, and if you ever want to come to Australia, we have a spare bedroom and live right near the beach and Scott will teach you how to surf!!

Kind regards,
Julie & Scott Randall

Desperate?

Yes we were. I would have offered to have his first-born if I wasn't 50 years old with a terminal disease *and* going through menopause.

Daniel responded the next day and said he would go back to the team and present our solutions, but this would not be for another week as that's when they were all back in town and would reconvene. That was frustrating but at least we were still hanging in there by the skin of our teeth.

I am a pretty determined person and I can never remember being so hell bent on anything in my life. I had to get to Portland. As hard as it would be on our family, I just had to get there. It would be a logistical and financial nightmare but something inside told me we had to go for it.

And it wasn't just me, the sensible monster was always saying to me, *There is something out there for you, Julie.* But now he was whispering in my ear, *It's going to be hard Julie, bloody hard, but that is where you need to be, you need to be in Portland for a chance of survival.*

We knew we had to wait a week, so I did my best to park it in the back of my mind.

I was still having chemo every two weeks and was pleased that the numbness in my fingers and toes had subsided. My instincts seemed to be working so far, so that's what I was running with. I was mindful that it was now halfway through November, and if my doctor was spot on with his prediction, the chemotherapy would be turning its back on me in about three months.

We all know how quickly twelve weeks goes by and try as I might, I couldn't stop the clock. I could not stop day from becoming night and the night becoming the morning, and with each day that passed I was a little closer to death if I didn't find a way to help my body repair itself.

I had a constant churning in my stomach. I was so envious of people who could just breeze through the day. Everyone has their issues and problems, I know, but trying to stay alive and save Scott and my girls from an unimaginable heartache was completely overwhelming. The thought of deteriorating into someone and something that I didn't know or recognise was beyond scary. The thought of my family watching that happen was gut-wrenching.

I had to find a way out. I just had to.

Chapter Thirteen

Letter to Mum in Heaven

Hi *Mum*,

How are you? What are you up to?

I haven't heard back but I'm guessing you must be busy coaching netball or playing Yahtzee.

Well *Mum*, I have good news and bad news. First of all, I had a brain tumour removed. Pretty heavy, I know, but it had to be done. It all went well and I'm okay.

Remember when we were little and we'd do something stupid and you'd say, 'You haven't got a brain in your head!' Well I can't vouch for the others, but I definitely do have a brain in my head and I now have proof. I can send you the scans if you don't believe me.

Anyway, Mum, the chemotherapy I have been on has worked, so that's a good thing! I've had some tumours disappear and the others have reduced. That's the good news, BUT the bad news is that apparently the tumours will soon build up a resistance and the treatment won't be working by March next year! It's only three and a half months away and that is scary stuff. But try not to worry, Mum. I'm not going to sit back and wait for that to happen. I won't!

Scott and I have been researching on the internet. Oh you probably don't know what that is. I have an idea; just look around for a guy called Steve Jobs and I'm sure he'll give you the heads-up on the world wide web. Can you ask him if you have Facebook up there please? It would be much easier to communicate that way.

Anyway, Mum, Scott and I found a clinical trial in Portland, Oregon. Yes I know, I don't know exactly where that is, either, and I don't care, I'd go to the moon if I had to. I just need to do something – and fast!

So this trial in America helps the immune system kick back into action and recognise the tumours and the cancer cells and destroy them without destroying the healthy cells like chemo does. We're talking to the people now, they've said no so far, but we won't give up. Mum, you know I have never been a quitter. Okay, yes, I did quit that judo class when I was nine, but those suits were hot and sweaty and the instructor was, well, how do I say this nicely? Okay, I've got it, a creep.

I miss you Mum. I still can't believe that someone you love so much can be taken from you like that. I just can't fathom it. I miss Nanna so much, too, Mum, do you see her? You were never too far away from each other. I'm guessing you guys play cards together.

Dad still misses you every day; he's 82 now and still very handsome. He hasn't met anyone else. He says no one compares to you. He just looks after all of us and his grandchildren.

Mark, Kerri, Michelle and Nicole are all good, Mum, great in fact. They've been there for me in the past five months as loyal and rock solid as ever. Michelle has had another bout but, as usual, she's come through it on top. We are all still married to our original partners which is a rarity these days, especially five out of five, but that's what you taught us. You used to say, 'If you marry someone and have kids, then that's it, you stay put no matter what.'

I remember one day challenging you on that, asking you, 'Okay, so what if they cheat on you?'

And you said, "Well if they do that you just shoot them."

You were so funny, Mum, and I'm guessing you still are. I bet you have all your mates up there in stitches. We grew up with that humour and I can't thank you enough because, boy, do I need it right now.

You and Dad gave us the best life growing up. I don't know if I ever thanked you. So I am now.

Pray for us Mum, me, Scott and the girls – we need your love and prayers more than ever. I need to be a part of this study in America. I know it with every fibre of my being.

Looking forward to hearing how you go with Steve Jobs.

I'll write again soon.

Love Jule xxx

Chapter Fourteen

I would wake up each morning after a very rough sleep, lie there for about two seconds and then it would come over me like a tidal wave – the realisation that I had advanced cancer and was facing a bleak future. I had to find a way to get myself into that study. I tried being a 'patient patient', knowing that the trial team would be meeting again in six days to discuss our situation, but I couldn't. I had to keep going. We had to keep on it. I had never been a narcissist, but it appeared I was becoming one – it was all about me. I told Scott that we needed to keep sending emails to show our commitment, that we were not going to let this go. So I fired off another email to Daniel Jackson:

Hi Daniel,

The more Scott and I talk about immunotherapy and the clinical trial in Portland the more we are sure that this is where we need to be. I do not have much time before the chemo will turn its back on me. I have two daughters and a husband who love me and need me. I have to give myself the best chance of survival. Daniel, you are my only link to a chance at life. Please convey to the team that we will do whatever it takes to get to Portland.

In your hands,
The Randalls

I knew I was being annoying and pushy, but I didn't care. While I was almost using emotional blackmail, I couldn't make it easy for them to say no. We needed someone on our side to fight for us and poor, unsuspecting Daniel Jackson from Portland, Oregon, inadvertently had my life in his hands. A woman he had never met who lived on the other side of the world.

In addition to pestering people, which had become my new vocation, I managed to stick to my diet and exercise regime to the letter. I did yoga, meditation and practised gratitude every day. I stared at my vision board and imagined my future – I was going to be in it. I was determined to see my girls get married and I was going to cradle their children in my arms. After I hit the send button and saw my message disappear, I threw on my exercise gear, whistled to Roxy and out we went into the park. Roxy chased the rabbits and I chased my future. I desperately wanted one so I ran and sang my song like I was already there.

I am happy and healthy,
All my organs have healed,
My body and its organs have healed,
I have faith in life.

I ran for half an hour that day, trying to clear my head and focus, singing the entire time. Then I went back inside and sat down next to Scott. 'We have to stop at nothing to make this happen. I want to live! We'll give them another 24 hours, then you need to send another email.'

'Okay I will,' he said reluctantly, probably also thinking we were now falling into the harassment category.

You won't be surprised that 25 hours did pass with no reply, and I got a little bee in my bonnet. Scott was upstairs in the bathroom so I walked over to his computer and clicked on his Sent Items. I was extremely annoyed to see that he had not sent another email to Portland, so I marched up the stairs and banged on the door. 'What are you doing in there? Haven't you got an email to send? We can't drop the ball, Scott, can you send it now please.'

'Yes dear,' was his response.

I waited until he had to go out to the post office a couple of hours later before I went stalking again. I clicked on the Sent Items tab and there was the email he'd promised to send:

Hi Daniel,

It's Scott Randall here, mate. I'm sorry to be bombarding you with all these emails.

I just wanted to say that we appreciate your help in trying to get us to Portland to take part in the PD-1 clinical trial.

Julie is my wife and my world and it eats away at me from the inside out to see her suffering like this, knowing what the future holds if she doesn't find a better way to treat her condition. She is the most strong and amazing woman I know, and the most loving and devoted mother to our two daughters. Everybody loves her, Daniel, and no one more than me. I can't bear the thought of not having her in my life. Our friends and family have had a fundraiser for us and we are able to send you whatever amount of money you need to ensure we have a spot in this trial.

Once again, thanks, mate, and I trust you will convey our willingness to the team.

The Randall Family

I always wondered what went through Scott's mind about me dying and being without me. Now I had seen it in writing. *Okay, so that's good,* I thought, *he made me cry, so let's hope he manages to pull at some heartstrings over in Portland. Good job, honey, I thought you just needed a little push.*

Daniel responded to both of our emails with. *'Will do.'*

After I sent another email and bullied Scott to do the same, he started getting a little testy. 'All right,' he said, 'but this is it until Daniel has a chance to meet with the others. He will think we are lunatics and change his email address.'

That's a point, I thought. So I reluctantly agreed to wait a few days.

Scott could see that I was starting to stress out and must have been thinking of a way to chill me out. That afternoon, out of the blue he suggested we go away for a few days, just to hang out and relax. Of course I agreed as I love any excuse to get away with him and thought we absolutely deserved it. I also figured it could be a belated anniversary present to ourselves. He booked us in to Kims Beach Hideaway in a little town called Toowoon Bay on the Central Coast of New South Wales. Kims is a special place for us – the place where Scott had proposed to me and the place we had celebrated our fifteenth wedding anniversary.

Kims Beach Hideaway dates back to 1886 and is full of history. It is a cluster of deluxe individual timber bungalows and villas on the beachfront but also built in a lush rainforest. It's such a unique and serene resort. The dining room is amazing and so is the food. You get your own special table where you sit for all your meals overlooking the ocean, which is usually aqua blue. I actually felt excited about going to Kims – I had almost forgotten what that emotion felt like. I knew I would still be in the same predicament but if I had to be in a predicament, then Kims was a nice place to be. We were staying in a villa called 'Tree Tops', which was totally private, with its own pool and spa surrounded by tropical gardens and views out to the horizon. We would be hidden away from the world, if only for a few days.

We drove up to Kims the next morning and arrived about lunchtime. The villa was lovely, even better than it looked online.

We couldn't wait to strip off, put on our cossies and laze around the pool, diving in to cool off at our leisure. Without giving too much away, we both love a skinny dip. But this time I had to do it with my hairpiece on, which was a bit sad and also an unwelcome reminder of my condition. Yes, I could have been brave and taken it off but my mind kept going back to that time on the Barrier Reef when Scott asked me 'not to go bald'. So I left well enough alone. Since we had complete privacy, we spent most of the time wearing very little. Now that *was* liberating.

When the meals were ready the bell would ring loudly. We dressed up and strolled down along the path down the steep hill, holding hands and trying to stay mindful because in that moment, everything was okay. The path was covered by Norfolk pines and led us all the way down to the restaurant to our special little table overlooking the ocean. The meals were buffet style, with prawns and oysters, salads and roasted vegetables, a selection of cold meats and of course steaks, chicken and fish with yummy sauces, most of which I could enjoy on my 'Bill' diet. We had a romantic meal, wandered back to our tree-top cabin, then Scott got out his guitar and we sang all the songs in our repertoire. After we had gone through our guitar songs we hooked the phone up to our portable speakers and played our favourite playlist.

Music and singing were the best escapes I had. When you're singing you are in the moment, in the song, connecting with the lyrics and imagining what the story meant to the songwriter. When the music hits you feel no pain. It was a welcome break from the all-consuming world of cancer and my obsession with securing the next piece in the puzzle, the jigsaw titled 'Julie Randall lives'. Singing and music are such beautiful things. It doesn't matter whether you're good or bad or mediocre. You can do it when no one's around and kid yourself you're pretty talented, that you should send off an application to *The Voice*.

Scott and I love our music; it has always been part of the glue that binds us together. Our favourite thing in the world is to sit on our back deck overlooking the park, have a barbecue and a few drinks on our own and sing along to our favourite songs. Some of our all-time favourites are 'Ordinary People' by John Legend, 'The End of the Innocence' by Don Henley, 'Up on the Roof' by James Taylor and Carole King, 'The Hard Way' by Keith Urban and 'Harvest Moon' by Neil Young.

I had promised myself I would not mention anything about cancer and/or Portland that night. I had to give Scott a break. But the next day would be another story.

We somehow managed to have fun and fell into our king-size bed at about midnight. I was awake half the night with night sweats. I didn't complain.

The bell rang in the morning and down the hill we went for an amazing gourmet breakfast. It was then that I got back onto the clinical trial bandwagon. I had given Scott a 24-hour reprieve, which for me was pretty good. I could tell he was enjoying the break. We had his laptop, so as soon as we got back to the villa, I checked our emails again, just hoping on the off-chance we might have received some good news.

There was an email there from Daniel Jackson, but it wasn't good news. He had managed to speak to the powers-that-be who had more or less dismissed us and pointed us back to a doctor in Newcastle, two hours from our home, whom he knew very well and thought may have some research studies coming up in Australia. They said they would email him and ask him to get in touch with us. I was livid.

We had already told them we had researched all the treatments and clinical trials here in Australia and that I qualified for none of them. The doctor he referred us to was a guy called George Bryant, a professor who was very highly regarded. That was fair enough, but if there was something for me in Australia we would have known about it. Our professor would have known about it. It would have been on the internet.

So, trying to refrain from sending a desperate, emotional email back to Daniel, I ran and jumped in the pool. I went under scarf and all and screamed loudly in my head. Then I got out of the pool, dried myself off and went back inside. I looked up George Bryant's number and called his office. He was busy of course, so I left a message with his secretary about a doctor in America who'd told me to contact him and that it was urgent. To my surprise about half an hour later, the phone rang and it was George. I tried to give him the very short version of my story so he wouldn't hang up on me and it worked. He listened intently. Then when I was finished he came out with these words: 'Portland, Oregon, is where you need to be.'

I said, 'Thank you, that's what I needed to hear,' and hung up. We were just going around in circles. I swore a lot, then jumped straight back onto the computer and sent another email.

Hi Daniel,

Thanks for your email. I have just called George Bryant and after a long conversation we both came to the same conclusion. I need to be in the PD-1 trial in Portland, Oregon. All roads point to you.

Please tell them that this statement came straight from Doctor Bryant's mouth. As for the financial part of it, we have it covered. We will not let money stand in the way of my survival.

Thanks for your help.

Julie Randall

Okay, so surely when they heard that the well-respected doctor from Australia was saying that's where I needed to be, they would stand up and take notice. Then just to give us another kick in the guts, we got an out-of-office reply from Daniel Jackson. He was away in Haiti for four days. My blood started boiling.

'He's probably gone off on stress leave,' Scott very kindly proclaimed, making me feel even worse. He then tried his best to convince me to chill out for a few days. That it would all work out. That Daniel Jackson would read my message when he got back and we would be given the green light. But I wasn't going to be happy until we were on that plane.

I had to regather; we were at a beautiful place, just the two of us, for three more days, and I had to try my best to stay in the moment and enjoy it. As hard as it was I managed to zip up my mouth and not mention cancer or clinical trials for the rest of our stay. For some reason while we were not talking about it

I felt that Scott was living in denial land, telling himself that everything would be okay and even if we didn't go to Portland that I would be fine. Telling himself I would be the only person in the world to survive this advanced, fast-moving stage four melanoma with only chemo as an aid.

I was wrong. He has told me since that he never stopped thinking about it. The fact that I could die and the mental torture I was going through. He says he went to bed thinking about it, he woke up thinking about it and then he thought about it all day long. He just put on a brave face for me, thinking that if he looked confident about my future then it would rub off on me. For all his little quirks and unusual behaviour, that man is the best thing that has ever happened to me. I can't describe in words how much I love him. I don't even think *he* knows. With a bit of luck he might read this memoir. But I wouldn't put my money on it. After all, he's a bloke and he already knows the ending.

Chapter Fifteen

Arriving home from our little getaway at Kims was bittersweet. I didn't want the magic to end, but I was also hanging out to see the girls and Roxy.

They were all happy to see us, especially Roxy, who performed her welcome-home dance with gusto. I didn't actually like being away from my family for too long. We were going through tough times, and it was important to be together as often as we could.

So, now I was home and time was ticking. I had to get back on the job. It had been almost four days, so hopefully Daniel, the head study nurse, would be back from leave.

I started feeling extremely nervous. What if they didn't want to put up with me and my antics for much longer and blocked me from all communications? I checked my email once more and there was nothing there.

So again I sat down and banged away at the keyboard.

Hi Daniel,

I hope you had a nice time in Haiti. I am just following up to see if you have had a chance to talk to the doctor in charge about my conversation with Doctor Bryant. As I explained he was adamant that your clinical trial in Portland is the one I need to be a part of, and fast. It is December now, Daniel, and I haven't got much time.

Please talk to the team again for me. There is nothing here in Australia that I qualify for. I think we have now established that as a certainty. It will be Christmas soon and I would love to cheer my family up with some good news.

Thanks again for your help and not blocking my email address.

Best wishes,
The Randall family

I pushed the send button, crossing my fingers and toes that I wouldn't get an out-of-office message. I didn't.

Yeah! That meant he was back at work.

I didn't hear anything for a day or two and was becoming increasingly uptight and irritable. Then it came, another email from Daniel stating the financial complications involved with overseas patients. He also mentioned that the trial was now at full capacity.

So there it was . . . another rejection.

Despair washed over me from my head to my toes. Scott tried to comfort me but this time not even he could console me. I put on my exercise gear and went for a run. I didn't know what else to do. I was jogging along, thinking, *How can these people do this to me, hadn't they taken an oath to help people who are dying?*

I despised admitting it, but apparently that was the deal, I was dying. I had been given a life expectancy of what, I wasn't sure. I was running along feeling as fit as a fiddle admitting to myself that I was dying. It didn't make sense.

I knew they had a drug over there in Portland that could potentially help me. They couldn't just dismiss me like that. Could they?

In that moment, I had an idea. I would remind them of that oath, the Hippocratic Oath. The one doctors take when they graduate. I turned around, headed straight back home and that's what I did.

I knew it was night-time in Oregon so I called and left a carefully rehearsed message on Daniel Jackson's answering machine. I wanted it to be my voice, not just words on an email.

'Hi Daniel, it's Julie Randall speaking, the serial pest from Australia. I am sorry that you have become the brunt of my frustrations, but as you can imagine I am beside myself sitting around waiting for my health to deteriorate and I am left alone to contemplate a fate that is almost beyond my imagination.

'I don't want to come across as a smart-arse, Daniel, but I have looked up the Hippocratic Oath that is taken by doctors and medical professionals. In a nutshell it says that "if" there is a treatment out there that may be able to help a person stay alive then any doctor with access to that medicine and authority to administer it is obliged to do so. Again, Daniel, the money is not an issue.

'Please go back to the team. I am just one little girl from Australia, I don't take up much room and I will volunteer and do whatever I can for the hospital, I promise.' I was talking very fast to make sure I could complete my carefully scripted message before I got the beep to cut me off.

I had read the Hippocratic Oath and it was quite longwinded, so I tried to relay the short version and sum up what it meant to me in layman's terms.

It was my last-ditch effort.

When I hung up, I was shaking and crying. I had told Scott what I planned to do and he wasn't a fan of the idea. So I couldn't go to him for comfort.

Then there was the waiting. But to my surprise, within 24 hours I received another email from Daniel.

Hi Julie,

I got your message. I will go back yet again to the team with your thoughts. Doctor Urba, who is leading the trial, is away for a week or so but I will talk to him again on his return and get back to you.

Regards,
Daniel Jackson

Still frustrating? Yes, but not dead in the water, so to speak. Waiting another week or so would be torture but I was used to torture. Bring it on!

I didn't tell Scott about the message, but I did mention that Daniel was still trying for us and it wasn't over yet.

Somehow I had to find a way of getting through the next week without sending any more harassing emails or making any desperate phone calls to Portland. It was two weeks before Christmas and again I resolved to stay firmly in the present. I wanted to enjoy Christmas with my friends and family, no matter what. I had to, because the mean monster repeatedly whispered in my ear that this Christmas might be my last.

As you know, I am a wife, a mum, a friend and a sister and Christmas shopping had to be done. I don't love shopping at the best of times, apart from secretly shopping for clothes online and pretending I've had them for ages. So, given my situation, Christmas that year was only going to make hitting the shopping mall even more excruciating.

Scott and I picked a day and headed out there. I will never forget that day and how I felt. I felt like an alien. Like everyone, even strangers, knew what was happening to me, then the reality of it hit me in the face. We walked into a homewares store not far from home. I'd decided we needed some new cushions to brighten up our home for Christmas. I love bright things, especially homewares, and I was doing anything I could to cheer myself up.

We were wandering around, happily distracted, when we bumped into a friend. Not a close friend, just someone we used to see from time to time. She had obviously heard about my condition and was visibly uncomfortable. 'How are you?' she asked with pity and sorrow all over her face. 'I've heard the dreadful news. What are you guys up to for Christmas? Not much I guess,' answering her own question. 'That was a silly thing to ask,' she continued nervously. 'I guess you won't be going away this year either. You poor things.'

Well that was it.

I had to do everything in my power to keep in control. I felt sick, I felt embarrassed and I felt helpless, standing right there in a beautiful store with bright colours and festive decorations everywhere.

Why anyone would feel compelled to say those things to me, to us, was beyond my comprehension. I could feel the tears welling and an anxious, breathless feeling rising up into my throat.

I turned my back on her and quietly motioned to Scott that I would be heading to the car. I don't know what he said to her, I didn't ask him. And that was my first and last Christmas shopping experience for 2012. I wouldn't even go to the supermarket; Scott did the groceries.

I know it can be a tricky situation when you bump into someone you know who has had a cancer diagnosis, but in my opinion, and it is just my opinion, why can't you just say, 'Hi, how are you?'

If the person wants to go into detail and divulge their story, it means they want to talk about it. But if they say, 'Good thanks, how are you?', then quite clearly they don't want to be in the middle of a store at Christmas being pitied and patronised and made to feel like a 'dead woman walking'.

Apparently people feel like they have to say something.

But why? What's wrong with, 'How are you?' Doesn't that cover all bases? Don't people with cancer deserve the same respect as everyone else?

Other people would stop me in the street and ask me where *all* of my tumours were.

'Can I ask why you need to know that?' I would respond, not caring if they felt a little awkward.

Another friend, a guy, told me that he saw me in the street one day just after hearing about my diagnosis, he didn't know what to say so he turned around and walked the other way.

I said, 'Good, I'd prefer that than you approaching me with a look on your face like you'd just bumped into a ghost.'

Once again that's just me and, like my husband, I can be a little weird. I know people mean well and some of them genuinely care and worry about you. But they say these things to you and then walk away and get on with their normal non-life-threatened lives. But for me, these invasive questions leave behind someone who is totally devastated and distraught.

Another week passed and no word from America. It was a week out from Christmas and the ants were jumping around in my pants like you wouldn't believe.

Will I send another email?

Maybe make another phone call?

Bloody hell, what should I do?

I couldn't make up my mind. Would I ask Scott? No, he would just say be patient, wait another day. I couldn't help myself, so I fired off another message.

Hi Daniel,

Julie here, have you had a chance to speak again with
Doctor Urba?

The Randalls

I liked to sign off with 'The Randalls', hoping to touch a nerve, that this wasn't just about me, it was about my whole family. To my surprise, he responded straight away to my email.

Hi Julie,

I did speak to Doctor Urba this morning and we are going
to speak to the finance department about your situation and
hope to have some feedback for you as soon as possible.

We also have a cut-off mark as the number of patients we
can accept in each trial so we will have to look at the situation
on that level as well.

Kind regards,
Daniel Jackson

Wow, okay, so there is still hope, I thought. This was definitely more promising than before. I felt a little more cheery. *Come on, you guys, just give us a figure and a date and we will be there; stop mucking around, let's just do this,* my mind was saying.

I decided to ignore the bit about the number of patients they accepted. I just couldn't bear the thought that this would be the next excuse to turn me down – if they had rules and regulations about the number of patients in a clinical study, then how was I going to win that battle?

Christmas Day arrived, a beautiful sunny day. The whole family gathered for breakfast and dinner as we did every year, 25 of us. It is family tradition that on Christmas Day, me, my sisters and brother along with our families get together in the morning and the evening and we all see our in-laws at lunchtime.

We also have a huge Boxing Day celebration. It was our Nanna Sharkey's birthday so my mum's side of the family would all get together at our home. Even though Mum and Nanna are not with us on earth anymore, we have kept that tradition sacred. My cousin Danny is a professional musician who sings and plays guitar, and the whole family has a singalong.

Scott and I and our girls practised a couple of songs that year – I was so excited to perform as a family. There we were, the four of us having a blast. It was hard for me to believe the situation I was in that Christmas, and I'm pretty sure my whole family felt the same.

I may never know what the rest of my family were thinking, but whatever their thoughts, they never showed them. They knew me and they knew I just wanted to be me, Julie. Sometimes I saw the worry written all over my dad's handsome face. I felt so bad that he had to bear this burden. I cannot even begin to imagine how I would be if this nightmare was happening to one of my girls, no matter how old they were. They will always be my babies.

We did go away that year, as always, to Crescent Head on the mid north coast of New South Wales. We go there every summer and have done since Morgan was a baby. It is just the perfect place for us, we love it. When the girls were little they had a ball running amok around the beach with their cousins. It has great waves for surfing, so Scott is in heaven whenever we go there; a beautiful creek that you can float down with the tide; a club; a pub; and a couple of cool restaurants. It was the most relaxing time of the year for us and I couldn't wait to get there.

I was still having chemo, so as usual my bald head was hidden away under a hairpiece and scarf. I decided to buy a bright-green, old-lady-style bathing cap – gorgeous! It looked ridiculous but I wanted to be able to immerse myself fully in the ocean without ruining my synthetic hair, so it was a necessary evil.

On our second day at Crescent, Scott and I decided to have a swim at a secluded beach. We love to dodge the crowds and soak up the feeling of space and serenity. The surf was quite rough that day and I had to dive under a massive wave that crashed down right in front of me. To my horror, the turbulence ripped my new green grandma bathing cap right off my head and it disappeared into the abyss. I screamed and put my hands up on my head hoping to cover up my baldness, but I'm pretty sure it wasn't working. Scott rescued the bathing cap and we managed to have a big belly laugh about it.

That day was the only time my husband saw me with no hair and it didn't seem to bother him one little bit. I remember thinking that perhaps he's not as shallow as I once thought.

Being on holiday didn't slow down my determination to get to Portland, so after a couple of days of bliss and sunshine I got back on the job. I asked Scott to check his emails and of course he obliged; by then he did what he was told. All of a sudden he started reading an email aloud.

Dear Julie & Scott,

Doctor Urba has agreed for you to send your case files over and we will assess them to ascertain if you are eligible to take part in our study.

We will need to look at your medical history and all of your scans and reports associated with your melanoma diagnosis to make sure you meet all of the strict study criteria. If you do, then we can move forward with working out a financial plan. No promises but fingers crossed.

Kind regards,
Daniel Jackson

Oh my god . . . they were seriously considering me.

I was ecstatic. Every cell in my body seemed to respond and dance in unison.

It wasn't definite, but it was the closest we had come to a 'yes' so far.

Scott had a big grin on his face – he loved to see me uplifted. I did a little happy dance accompanied by a loud scream and then of course I had a cry. This was my only hope and I felt we were now one step closer to getting a drug I had a chance of responding to. I didn't know what the 'strict criteria' were, but I would find a way to meet them.

We got straight onto the task at hand, sending out emails to doctors, hospitals, professors and surgeons requesting all my files. We had to compile them and get them over to Portland as soon as possible, to strike while the iron was hot.

Finally, we had some hope, hope that I may stay alive a little longer.

I wasn't ready to die. I had too much to live for.

Chapter Sixteen

Scott and I were glad to say goodbye to 2012. With a spring in our step and hope in our hearts we tried hard to enjoy the rest of our summer holiday.

On the way home in the car, all I could think about was getting my medical files over to America. I'd nervously looked at the criteria for eligibility and to the best of my knowledge I was a candidate.

Advanced disease – check

Disease in major organs – check

No active brain tumours (that I knew about) – check

I had to hope and pray that nothing new had appeared on my brain because if there was any sign of a tumour I would not be considered. I couldn't give energy to that, I just had to press on.

Now you would think that getting hold of your own personal medical history would be a fairly straightforward task, wouldn't you? Well, it wasn't.

We had to order them and then pay a fee, around $60, to access *my* records from the archives. Archives, I thought, it's only been six months. Then we were told it would probably take about a week to get our hands on them as most of the staff were still on leave. I was pissed off but Scott was ropeable.

It was unnerving listening to Scott's conversation with one of the nurses at the hospital demanding we get the files immediately. I thought I was going to see smoke billowing from the top of his head.

He was emphasising the fact that we needed the files immediately, because we only had a small window of opportunity to convince the head doctor in Portland that I was a suitable candidate. And that my life depended on it.

The trial was almost at full capacity and we needed to show our commitment. She knew our situation and how desperate we were; it was the same chemo nurse who had said to me right at the beginning that they would try to keep me alive until a clinical trial became available.

But even with that knowledge she didn't seem willing to go the extra mile for us. Scott went off like a firecracker – while he was driving. He yelled down the phone at her and I was cringing in the passenger seat. He finished the call by saying, 'We want those files. I will be there at twelve o'clock tomorrow to pick them up and they'd better be ready.'

I had never heard him talk like that to anyone in the 25 years I had known him. The stress he was feeling was palpable, it was consuming his whole being. Like me, he was aware that as every day passed, we were one step closer to March. I knew he was scared, I could feel it.

The next day we drove to the hospital to pick up the files and funnily enough, they were ready. Sometimes tantrums do the trick. We went straight to the post office and express-posted them to the Providence Cancer Center in Portland.

I remember thinking that day how crazy it was, walking around like everybody else, blending into society. None of the people I encountered would have had a clue what was going on in my body or inside our heads. No one in that post office would have known I had just sent off a package that could ultimately determine if I lived or died.

I guess that goes for all of us. The outside shell is sometimes a far cry from what's happening on the inside. We put up walls and barriers to protect us from others seeing our vulnerabilities and our fears. I had become the epitome of that.

Acting like everything was okay was my way of coping. I wanted to become what I focused on, an alive, living, breathing specimen of wellness. I would become what everyone else saw on the outside. I felt strongly that with some help I could also make that happen on the inside.

Daniel Jackson hadn't indicated how long it would take for the powers-that-be to make a decision on my eligibility, so I had to *try* to be a little more patient this time. A clinical study basically means you become a lab rat to be studied for the purposes of science, but I saw it a little differently. For me it was a chance to stay alive and if I helped science in the process, then happy days.

I felt it was time to tell the girls what we were up to. We owed it to them to let them know what we had been working on for the past two and a half months. We needed to gauge how they felt about the fact that their mother might be leaving home to go to the other side of the world. That their mum wanted to be part of a clinical trial with an experimental drug that only offered about a 38 per cent chance of response and no guarantee of long-term results.

I was dreading this conversation but it had to be done. I rehearsed my speech over and over again in my mind but when it was crunch-time and the girls were at home it went something like this.

'Girls, can we have a little talk?'

They both walked towards me with fear in their eyes.

'You both know that I'm on chemotherapy and it's working, it's keeping things under control, right?'

'Yes,' they responded in unison.

'Well, apparently there is a big chance that it will stop working in the next couple of months.' I hated watching the horrified looks appear on their beautiful little faces.

They stayed silent and I went on. 'Dad and I have done a lot of research and we have found a clinical trial that can offer me another treatment option.'

'What's a clinical trial?' they asked.

'That means a group of patients go on a drug that is experimental but is having some promising results and they are monitored throughout the trial to help scientists come up with treatments to help save people's lives. The medical people involved are hopeful that this drug can bring long-term responses to patients like me and it would be far less harmful to my body than the chemotherapy drugs. This treatment is working for a third of the people involved in the study. It's not a certainty but it is a possibility and one I feel strongly about.'

'That's good, Mumma,' Morgan said, her face a lot less strained.

Remy looked intrigued, in a good way.

I continued. 'Dad and I have been working very hard to get a place in the trial and they only have limited spots. We've reached the point where they've asked us to send over my medical files to see if I qualify.'

'Over where?' Remy asked

I paused and then burst into tears. 'America.'

'*America!*' Morgan responded.

'Yes Morgs,' I managed to blurt out, 'but if it has a chance of keeping me well long term then I feel strongly that I, we, need to give it a go. There is nothing here in Australia that I qualify for. Dad and I have looked at every angle.'

'How do you know it will work?' Remy piped in.

'I don't know for sure but I just have to try.'

'How long do you have to go for?' Remy asked.

I didn't have the heart to say two years, so I stumbled my way through the answer to her question. 'Well, I'm not really sure but I would say at least six months, if it's working. I just need to get myself there and then find a way to get back home to you guys.'

'Whereabouts in America?' Morgan asked, this time a little more enthusiastic. 'LA?'

She loves her dancing and she knows there are amazing dance workshops in LA. Kids are funny.

'No,' I said, 'Portland, Oregon.'

'Where?'

'Portland in the state of Oregon. I'm not exactly sure where that is and I'm not even going to look at a map until we get the green light, because it doesn't matter where it is. It's where I need to be.'

I stopped crying, then I just simply asked, 'What do you guys think about that?'

'If it's going to make you better, Mumma, of course we want you to go.' Morgan took control and answered for the both of them.

We had a group hug and then we all cried again. Even after all these months none of us could conceive what was happening to our family and how our once wonderfully, joyful chaotic lives had come to this.

It was the second hardest conversation I had had with my girls since this ordeal began. I was standing in front of them admitting that the chemotherapy was not the answer. It was not going to cure me. I had lulled them into a false sense of security: my bright and breezy manner and my positive attitude had made them believe all would be fine, and now I was admitting it wasn't.

Scott and I were new at this game, we didn't know the right way to play it. I didn't have my mum on earth anymore to help me wade through these very stormy waters. I just went with my gut instincts. I wanted to protect them from the fear, the scariness of what might happen to their mum and the unbearable thought that they may have to go through the rest of their lives without her.

I had mixed emotions about that afternoon. While I had finally come clean about the severity of my condition, I had thrown them back into turmoil. Plus, there was a chance that I wouldn't be accepted, and then what? What could they cling to? *Bloody hell, what have I done?* I remember thinking after that conversation.

Later that day I told Scott about my conversation with the girls and he was proud of me. He knew I'd been dreading it. Then I broke it to him that I didn't quite tell them that if we got the go-ahead he would be coming with me, at least for a few weeks until I settled in.

I knew my girls well and they wouldn't want both of us so far away in these scary times. Things were already tough enough. They also had to put up with people permanently asking them questions. The poor kids. I really wished people would leave them alone. I wanted to buy them T-shirts saying, 'Please don't ask me about my mum, I am a kid and I don't want to be reminded about it when I am trying very hard to live my life like a normal person.'

I know people are concerned, but they just don't realise the impact even a simple question can have. People would also try to drill down to get more information about my condition. It was so upsetting for my girls, and they didn't know how to answer the intrusive questions. If I went to America they would be hammered with questions and it broke my heart. I took my girls to a psychologist – a beautiful lady named Marianne – to help them cope with the collateral damage this situation was causing. I had become close to Marianne – she had helped me through my grief when my mother passed away.

Scott knew how hard it was for me to tell the girls that day, so he decided to surprise me with tickets to see Carole King, one of my all-time favourite singers. The tickets were for a weekend in the Hunter Valley, two hours away in the beautiful wine country. He knew I would be excited about seeing Carole perform and he was trying everything he could to distract me from Portland and my obsession to stay alive. Anyone who has been in this position will know that it is almost impossible to think about anything else.

He handed me the tickets with a tender, lingering kiss on the forehead. He then told me that our best friends Brad and Liz were coming and so was my sister Michelle and her husband, Kevin. I think I even jumped up and down with excitement.

———

Waiting, waiting, waiting, and no word from Portland. I was so uptight that my heart was racing permanently. I sent an email asking if they had received the files and again I got a bounce-back. Daniel Jackson was out of the office for another week.

I was gutted, ranting and raving, not knowing where to turn or what to do. Even Roxy ran away and hid in the shower recess, her favourite hiding spot.

That's it, I thought, *they were just humouring me, they had no intention of accepting me. They were so sick of me pestering and harassing them that they just asked me to send over the files so they could find an excuse to rule me out and get rid of me once and for all. What an idiot I was to think they would take me.*

I went to our room and started bawling like a baby. The out-of-office auto reply was saying it all. They didn't care, I was just some silly desperate woman from Down Under. I was totally and utterly inconsolable.

Then an hour later that same morning, I was walking around aimlessly, after venting my frustrations on Scott and my dad, when the home phone rang. I didn't want to answer it, thinking it was going to be someone from the Philippines telling me my computer was going to die unless I carefully followed their instructions and gave them my personal banking information. Now that would have really pissed me off.

Anyway, something made me pick up the phone and bark 'Hello' into the receiver. Then I heard a female voice; it was an American accent.

'Halllooo, is that Julie?'

'Yes,' I replied hesitantly.

Then the voice said, 'This is Patti from Providence Cancer Center in Portland.'

'Yeesss,' I said as my heart skipped a beat.

'What day would you like your appointment with Doctor Urba, Monday the 25th of February or Monday the 4th of March?' She said it like she was a receptionist from the local dental surgery trying to set up an appointment for a scale and clean.

Holy shit, my heart started racing and my head was spinning. I had a hundred different thoughts racing around my mind. I couldn't believe what I was hearing.

'Can I talk to my husband and call you back please?' I stammered.

'Suuurrre,' said Patti. 'I'll send you an email with the options.'

Was I dreaming? I pinched my arm hard. No I wasn't. It really did happen. I wasn't expecting that! I was going. Oh my god. They were taking me. They were giving me a chance at life. My mind started going crazy. *I love you Patti, whoever you are. I love you and when I get over there I am going to squeeze the life out of you. Because you have just said the best words I have ever heard in my life.*

So there it was, after what seemed like a million phone calls, countless emails, ten buckets of blood, sweat and tears . . .

WE WERE GOING TO PORTLAND, OREGON, wherever the hell that was!

Chapter Seventeen

I finally dragged myself off the floor after collapsing in a heap and weeping uncontrollably for a myriad of reasons. I pulled myself together and made a phone call to my husband who was in his car at the time. I asked him to pull over.

'What's wrong?' he asked, sounding slightly perturbed.

'We're going to Portland.'

Then after what seemed like forever, he responded. 'You're kidding me. I can't believe it.' He didn't react quite like I did and I totally understood why. I could tell he was stunned. This was a surreal situation. I imagined all of the emotions that would have started stirring up inside him, good and bad. The good part was obvious. The bad part would be leaving the kids and trying to work out the logistics of such an operation.

Then he congratulated me for my tenacity and said he was proud of me. I have always loved it when he tells me this, and that moment was the best of all.

I went to my computer to see if the email from Patti had arrived. I needed to see her words in writing to believe it was really true. I hit the send/receive button and there it was, an email giving us two options for the next appointment, 25 February or 4 March, to meet the head study doctor, Walter Urba. Wow! Then I noticed there was an attachment titled 'Julie Randall – Patient Payment'. It was from the financial department asking us to transfer US$20,000 to a specified bank account.

A little shocked? At first I was, but then I regathered and thought that this was a small price to pay if it prolonged my life. In any case it wasn't payment for the treatment, it was there in case I became ill and had to be hospitalised. And we did tell them that money was not an issue. Thanks to my amazing family and friends who held the fundraiser for us, we did have that amount of money sitting untouched in the bank ready to go.

Then later that day I received another message requesting that I go off my current treatment, as my body had to be completely free of the chemotherapy drugs before I could take part in the trial. Now that was a scary thought. The chemo had brought me to this point and for that I was grateful. Although we knew it wasn't going to last, it was still working. But what choice did I have? I would have to take the biggest leap of faith I could ever imagine and stop my chemotherapy infusions.

I had to start making decisions on dates and of course break the news to the girls. It still wasn't a done deal that I was in – I had to have up-to-the-minute MRI scans on my arrival in Portland to make sure my brain was free of tumours. That's how quickly things can happen in my condition. I could have a scan here in Australia and send the results, but they would not take them as gospel in case any tumours had appeared between here and the US. The tests would have to be done over there and if something showed up we would be packing our bags and flying home to a fate I did not want to contemplate.

I called my family and asked them to pass on the good news to my close friends. Everyone was happy. They knew it was what I wanted, but I also got the impression most of them thought it was a long shot. I understood how they felt. Most people would have thought that at my stage of the big C, I had little hope of survival. I thought differently, I had to.

The conversation I was dreading the most was the one in which I would tell my daughters that I was going to Portland and taking their father with me. I was struggling to believe this had become a reality, even though I had pushed so hard for it. Getting to Portland had occupied my every waking moment *and* most of my sleeping ones as well. If I wasn't thinking about it I was dreaming about it.

I started to freak out. I had to get into the fresh air, so Roxy and I went to the park for a run. I sang my song, this time with renewed vigour. I was pumping up my body, saying *'Come on!'* like Lleyton Hewitt on centre court. I was thanking it for keeping me well and getting me that far. I told my body I was taking the chemo away so it would have to keep strong and keep me healthy until I arrived in America and gave it something new to help it repair itself. Hopefully for good.

No matter how hard I tried, however, I couldn't stop the monsters, all of them, from climbing aboard. The nice one was really happy for me and congratulated me on my determination and persistence. The sensible monster was being practical as always and wondered how we would manage the financial situation. He asked how Scott could afford to be away from his business for an extended length of time. He said, *No matter what you're going through, Julie, you still have to earn an income and pay your mortgage.* The mean one, as usual, was trying his best to rain on my parade. He piped in during my song and said, *Do you really want to leave your girls and go all the way over to the other side of the world for an experimental treatment? What if it doesn't work and you are spending your last precious days away from them?*

I burst into tears and spent the last ten minutes of my run bawling my eyes out. Composing myself on my way back home, I reminded him in a very curt manner, *For god's sake, I am doing this for them. Don't you get it? There is nothing in Australia to help me. I'm going so I can have a future with them.*

It was going to be tough, but we would all have to eat a bag of cement and harden up. This was our best chance to keep our precious family together on this earth for a lot longer, hopefully much longer than predicted by the medicos.

We chose 4 March for our meeting with Doctor Urba. By then I would have been off the chemo for six weeks and the drugs would be well and truly out of my system.

I delivered the news to my girls one by one, becoming a blubbering mess on both occasions. They were so brave about it and I could tell they shared my renewed sense of hope. Morgan said, 'That's great news, Mumma,' and gave me a big hug. Remy tucked her little head into my neck, which made my heart sink to the floor and then I felt anger. My poor little baby, she had just broken up with her boyfriend of two years under not very nice circumstances and was also trying to deal with that. So I decided not to tell them about Scott coming too. That would just have to wait for another time.

So, now it was actually confirmed we were going to Portland, Oregon, I started researching the place to find out where it was. I had heard it mentioned from time to time over the years, so I delved into my subconscious and pictured it right in the middle of America, but I could not have been further off the mark. I was never very good at geography and even though I had spent two months travelling in the US in my early twenties with my friend Irene, I still had no idea.

I found out Oregon is north of California on the Pacific North West Coast and Portland is in the far north of Oregon, just south of Washington State. It certainly wasn't renowned for its good weather and at the time didn't seem to be much of a tourist destination. It was popular for its microbreweries and only an hour or so from the coastline, which brightened my diehard surfie husband's spirits a little. I didn't tell him that for eleven months of the year it was too cold to venture into the ocean. I needed him to be excited about something. The live music culture was huge and as you know we love our music, so that was another bonus. It looked like there were some beautiful things to see if you ventured out of the city. I prayed I would stay well enough to see them.

In all of this mayhem, the much-anticipated Hunter Valley weekend was upon us. It would be a welcome break and hopefully a distraction from the crazy world we were in.

We drove up with my sister Michelle and her husband, Kevin, in a convoy with our friends Liz and Brad. Arriving on the Friday afternoon, we girls went to the spa while the boys played golf. We had a beautiful dinner in our hillside cabin overlooking the green hills with a couple of wineries in the distance. It was stunning. Everyone knew about the up-and-coming mission to the US, but no one talked about it that night, we were all having too much fun. We played old music and reminisced about the past, and soon it was two in the morning.

On Saturday, concert day, we all woke up a little the worse for wear after the excitement of the night before. But we just had to shake it off because we had front-row seats. Liz had made a reservation for lunch at a gorgeous restaurant at Peterson House in a picturesque vineyard setting. It was just divine and the perfect way to experience the true essence of the valley.

After lunch we headed back to our cabins and dolled ourselves up for the concert. We were all secretly hoping James Taylor would make a guest appearance, as someone had heard a rumour that he would be. At around 4pm we hopped on the courtesy bus, which transported us to the venue. The bus was full of drunk couples in their 50s and 60s who had obviously been very excited that day, just as we had been the night before. I couldn't help but wonder what state they would be in on the way home. It was very funny.

Our seats were fabulous. There was no sign of James Taylor, but Carole was amazing. She wasn't quite as sharp as she had once been, but hey, the woman was 71. She sang all our favourites that night – 'Up on the Roof', 'Smackwater Jack' and 'Natural Woman', among many others. She chose to end the night with one of her classics, 'So Far Away'. As soon as the song began I just lost the plot. Michelle was next to me, and she put her arm around me, cradling my head on her shoulder. I was gasping for air between sobs as the reality hit me. I was moving away from home, my family and my friends to the other side of the world under these crazy circumstances. I looked up at Michelle and she was trying to sing along to the song. I put my head up and in between sobs I whispered in her ear. 'You are in denial, aren't you? You don't believe I'm going?' She burst into tears and we both cried our eyes out.

The bus ride home was hilarious. Most of the original drunk passengers, as predicted, were completely hammered. One extremely pissed woman actually threw up in her handbag. The rest of them tried to recreate Carole's tunes, unsuccessfully. They were going to get their money's worth come hell or high water.

I remember that weekend, every second of it. It was my last taste of real fun before going home and getting myself together to tackle my future.

I made an appointment with my local doctor to tell him what we were doing and explained that I would be taking myself off the chemo. He suggested I have one more infusion as that would still give me four weeks for the drug to be out of my system. He also told us to be careful going through Customs in the US as they have been known to deny people entering the country for medical reasons.

Did he have to say that? Really? That would be the living end. Doing all the hard work and paying all that money, to be turned away when we arrived. That just wasn't going to happen. It couldn't, I had to keep telling myself.

Besides his warning, he was actually quite encouraging about our venture and said that if I was lucky enough to respond to the drug, it could be promising in the long term. He congratulated us on getting ourselves into the study and wished us good luck. And that was the last time I ever laid eyes on him.

I didn't have the next chemo infusion as he suggested; I had to make sure I was drug free. It was totally unnerving but totally necessary in the big picture.

Thursday 28 February 2013 snuck up on us. It was the day before we were due to fly out of the country. We had booked our flights and our accommodation for the first couple of weeks. Beyond that, we had no clue what we would be doing; we would work that out later. I had already plucked up the courage and told the girls I needed their dad with me for at least a few weeks. They were upset but they understood that it would be too traumatic for me to get on the plane alone. Our girls were twenty and seventeen; they were just babies, really, *my* babies, and I was leaving them to fend for themselves. Family and friends would be watching out for them and having them over for dinner and to stay whenever they wanted. But in their hearts they would be lonely and scared, and that cut me like a knife.

Unsurprisingly, I hadn't been sleeping much and was still dealing with the night sweats. I had a constant, horrible gnawing in my stomach. I did not want to leave my babies, but I had to. I had to go away short term for a chance to be with them long term – that's what I told myself over and over again. Every time I thought about it, I broke down. Life had been a non-stop cry fest for the previous two weeks.

The thought of leaving Remy was tearing my heart out. She had been suffering from acute anxiety brought on by my diagnosis and her break-up. It was all too much for her to deal with. You could see it in her eyes. How could we leave her to deal with this alone? I started to doubt if I would actually get on the plane.

Then, on that Thursday evening, the night before we left, I walked into Remy's room. She was lying on her bed and I could tell she was in a bad way. She had been suffering from the anxiety and she now had a terrified look in her eyes. When I asked her what was wrong, apart from the obvious, she said, 'I can't do this, Mum, I can't stay here without you.'

So without hesitation I just said, 'Okay, you'll have to come with us. We'll find a way for you to do your schoolwork over there.' I went downstairs, told Scott and he agreed. He logged on to his computer and booked her on our flight to LA, and I booked her on the flight from LA to Portland on my computer. We were so lucky – there was room on both flights. She was coming.

My feelings at that time were a mixture of frustration and relief. I was annoyed that my condition was having such an impact on her life. It was her final year at school, a time when she should be creating a future for herself. On the other hand, I was actually elated that she would be with us and not at home without her mum and dad. Thank goodness she had a current passport.

Of course, this would now mean leaving Morgan on her own. I can't explain in words what that time was like. We were all beside ourselves and as usual Scott had to be the strong one and talk us all through our dreadful situation. Morgan put on a brave face and waited until we were alone, saying, 'It's probably better if she goes, Mum. I think the best place for her is with you and Dad.'

'Thank you god, whoever and wherever you are, for giving me such an amazing child,' I remember saying out loud. Morgan smiled wearily.

It was 1 March 2013 and I had to say goodbye to my first-born daughter, not knowing when or if I would see her again. We were all up early, including Morgan, who had to teach a before-school dance class that day. The three of us had to leave home at 7am to allow for traffic or other disturbances on our drive to the airport for our 11.30am flight. We could not miss that plane to America. We were being picked up from home by the airport bus and it was about 7.05am when I saw it stop outside our house. My heart started racing as I watched the driver walking down the driveway to help us with our bags. *This is it*, I thought. *I now have to say goodbye.* I went up to Morgan's room, where she was sitting on her bed. Sitting down next to her, I tried so hard not to lose it completely.

'Bye Moo,' I said.

'Bye Mumma,' she said in a soft, sad voice.

I went on. 'I love you so much. I will miss you so much and thank you so much for being so strong and so understanding. I promised you I would fix this way back in the beginning and that is what I am going to do.' I was howling by then and she was comforting me.

'I know you will, Mumma, I am so proud of you.'

I just had to keep my promise to my beautiful daughter. I kissed her on the forehead and left the room. I went downstairs cuddled Roxy, walked out the door and I was gone. I left Scott and Remy to say goodbye. We were on our way to Portland, Oregon, on the other side of the world, leaving some very, very precious cargo behind.

Chapter Eighteen

The drive to the airport was horrendous. The closer we got, the closer I was to a treatment that might keep me alive, but further away from my beautiful girl who had been left at home without her mum, dad and sister under such hideous circumstances.

I had to trust that the mothering I had done so far would help her stay strong and find a way to get through this incredibly challenging time. When they handed me my much longed-for baby girl at 11.45am on Friday 4 September 1992, I envisaged a beautiful life for her. Thank god I couldn't see the future.

I had signed up to the trial for two years, if I made it that far. That was the deal. The Portland medical team had made this very clear from the start and of course I had gone along with it. Two years away from my family and friends was incomprehensible, but we had to take things one day at a time. In my head I had to cut this excursion down into bite-size chunks. That was the only way I could handle it.

It was a Friday, and Sydney airport was busy as usual. The three of us were doing what we had to do – lining up in queues, showing passports and having our bags weighed. I felt so sorry for Remy, she must have been wondering what on earth she was doing there; I felt so much guilt for the chaos I had created for my precious little family.

After we checked the bags we made our way through Customs and then to the security screening machines. I don't know why, but I'm always nervous going through those machines, like I'm a drug smuggler or a terrorist just waiting to be found out. Scott and Remy breezed through, but of course not me, I was bailed up.

'Could you take your hat off please, Ma'am,' one of the lovely security fellows said at the top of his voice.

I didn't want to yell out and tell the world that I was bald and my hair was fake and if I took off my hat there would be a hairpiece with my plaits attached and that my nude nut would be sticking out the top. So I tried to whisper it to him to deflect unwanted attention.

'Excuse me, Ma'am,' he yelled again.

So I had to say it a little louder. 'I'm bald and wearing a hairpiece and I don't want to take my hat off.'

He finally got it. He patted my head like he was patting a dog to make sure I didn't have any weapons of mass destruction hiding underneath my cap. He seemed satisfied and finally waved me through.

In a daze, the three of us sat down at one of the airport cafés and tried to eat some breakfast. Scott kept his eye on the monitors and all too soon we were called to board the Qantas flight to LA, a thirteen-hour journey to the other side of the world. We would then board another flight to take us up to Portland, a place that was foreign to us yet so important to our future.

I felt numb; it was like my mind was trying to shut down because it couldn't take any more thoughts. Even the mean monster knew better than to get on the plane with me that morning because he knew that if he started with his antics there was a big chance I would unbuckle my belt, jump out of my seat, run off the plane and sprint all the way home to my daughter. Although, I had my suspicions that the mean monster would find his way to Portland.

The nice monster did try to perk me up that morning by saying, *Come on, girl. You've got this. It's what you want, remember? This is what you have fought so hard for, for the past three months – let's do this!* I did take a little comfort from his encouragement that day.

Scott and I had originally booked an exit row because of my claustrophobia – I need room for my legs and a feeling of space otherwise I could have a severe panic attack. Incredibly, there was a spare seat next to Scott and me, so Remy could sit with us. I thanked the universe for that spare seat – it meant Scott could sit next to me on the flight rather than taking Remy's seat. I needed to be stuck to Scott like glue. I have never been a clingy person; in fact if you ask anyone who knows me they would say I am exactly the opposite. But in those tumultuous times I had almost become like a leech. I would have been happy if we were joined at the hip like Siamese twins, but I guess that would have been a little tricky on the flight. When Scott was close I could somehow cope.

So there we were, in the exit row right opposite the cabin crew who were strapped in and ready for take-off *and* ready for a chat.

'Where are you guys going? Staying in LA or going somewhere else?' one of them asked.

'We're going to Portland,' Scott said, hoping he didn't have to elaborate.

'Portland,' the flight attendant echoed with obvious surprise in his voice. 'It's very grey and dreary there at this time of year. What's taking you to Portland?'

I just sat there and let Scott stutter and stammer his way through the answer. 'We just thought we'd go and have a look,' he said, sounding a little bit silly.

The flight attendant then went on to tell us about some tourist attractions and things we should see, but we were not interested; it all went straight over our heads.

Playing tourists was the last thing on our minds that morning. Then it came, the roar of the engines, rolling down the tarmac, picking up more and more speed and then that *ba-bom* as the back wheels lifted off the ground and we were up into the sky. The truth was, I didn't really know for sure if I would ever come home.

After a long and tedious flight we landed in LA at 7am, all of us shattered. LA airport was manic and the queue to get through security was about two kilometres long. Well, maybe not two kilometres, but very bloody long. Then suddenly it washed over me like a tsunami – the conversation with the oncologist about going to the States for treatment.

'Remember,' he said, 'sometimes they stop you at security and deny you entry if you say you are in the US for medical treatment.'

Well that was it. I started sweating and shaking and my heart was almost pounding out of my chest. I whispered to Scott, reminding him of that conversation.

I had successfully blocked it out until that moment.

He said, 'Don't worry, darl, we'll be right.'

But I could see a little concern appear in his beautiful blue eyes. As we got closer I could see the faces of the men and women in their booths stamping passports. They looked angry, all of them. They mostly had moustaches, except for the women. Not from that distance anyway, but I reserved my judgement until we got a little closer. What they did have in common was that 'don't mess with me' look all over their faces.

I didn't want to lie about why we were there because I was scared to death they would somehow find out and kick my sorry butt all the way back to Australia. We'd edged closer and closer to the front of the line when a short, stocky guy called, 'Next!' and motioned us towards him.

'Are you a family?' he sternly asked.

'Yes,' we all said together.

'What are you doing in the States?'

This was it, the question I had been dreading. 'I'm here for medical treatment. I've been accepted into a clinical trial.'

'Whereabouts, Ma'am?' he asked, staring at my passport then looking back up at me about five times as I answered his question.

'I've got a horrible wig on in that photo,' I said, trying to break the ice.

But his expression didn't change, he just kept staring at me and then after what seemed like a decade he finally said, 'Put your finger on the screen, Ma'am, and look at the camera.'

I did what I was told, then he said, 'Thank you, Ma'am, good luck with your treatment.'

I burst into tears and walked through the booth extremely relieved but very emotional. Then I waited for Scott and Remy. We were all allowed into the country. It was a good start.

We didn't have a lot of time until the flight to Portland, so we walked briskly down to the other end of the airport. There was no time for fluffing about and before we knew it, we were on the plane.

Scott and Remy were together in one row and god knows how, but I was stuck in the middle in the row behind them, thinking *How the hell did this happen?*

Remy looked quite comfortable sitting next to her dad, so I was trying to stay cool and not make a fuss. But I was sweating and shivering and it all got on top of me. Just as the plane was about to take off I unbuckled my belt and jumped out of my seat. The hostess ran towards me and asked me what I was doing.

'I can't sit there, I just can't. I'll have to swap with my husband.'

Scott and Remy looked up at me with mortified looks on their faces.

Looking extremely annoyed, Scott got up and swapped seats with me. Obviously by that stage he was tired and irritable.

It was a two and a half hour flight, which seemed like nothing after the thirteen hours we had just endured. We were all glad our journey was almost over.

The flight was pretty smooth and as we were getting closer to landing, I distinctly remember the captain announcing, 'We have just started our descent into Portland and the weather is, well, just like most days in Portland, cold, cloudy and raining.'

'Bewdy,' I said to Remy. 'Doesn't look like we'll be working on our tans over here.'

She responded with a little chuckle, all she could muster after the sixteen-hour journey.

We arrived in Portland on schedule. I remember thinking the airport was lovely, clean and bright. Not how I'd pictured it. I had no idea how familiar I would become with that place.

We claimed our bags and walked across the road to the cab rank. The pilot wasn't kidding when he said it was cloudy, gloomy and raining, but it wasn't as cold as I'd expected. We hopped into a cab and headed into the city, and as I stared out the window, all of a sudden a huge white sign on the side of an old red brick building caught my eye. 'PROVIDENCE'. It made my stomach drop. It turned out that Providence is a massive organisation with buildings all over the city. That was the organisation I was trusting with my life, literally! It felt weird to be in a city I had begged and pleaded to be part of, yet it felt foreign, strange and unwelcoming.

We had booked a room with a fireplace at the Marriott Residence Inn on Multnomah Street for the first few nights. It was important to me to have a fireplace. There is something therapeutic and comforting about staring into a fire, watching flames dancing around. This became a common pastime for me, pretty much my meditation practice.

The cab pulled up outside the hotel, around two in the afternoon. It was just a stone's throw away from the city centre. The season had just changed from winter to spring, and just like that famous verse in the Mamas and Papas song, all the leaves were brown and the sky was grey.

We left Sydney on Friday 1 March 2013 and arrived in Portland on the same day. Having given ourselves two days' grace to make sure there were no hiccups, we were more than ready for our appointment on 4 March at 8am.

We checked in at the hotel reception, then went straight to our room, put down our bags, jumped into our king-size bed and crashed out. Scott on the right, me on the left and Remy in the middle, and that's how we slept for the next four weeks.

There were a few little implications with those sleeping arrangements which I don't think need any further explanation, but things were far from normal, so that's the way it was. My baby girl needed to be as close to us as possible. And that was all right by me.

We all started to rouse from our sleep at around 7pm. Since it was night-time we were all feeling odd and it was only then that we noticed the loud noises at regular intervals and realised we had a busy train line directly behind us. Scott mentioned that it could become annoying, but for me it was low on my worry list.

We decided we were starving and had no clue where to go for food, so we went for a walk to see what we could find. It was surprisingly mild that night and I remember only having to wear a leather jacket, red to be precise, over my jeans and T-shirt. Those times are indelibly stamped into my consciousness.

We walked out onto the street and to say we were discombobulated doesn't do the word justice. After wandering around aimlessly we stumbled across Applebee's Grill and Bar, one of a chain of family restaurants with a Mexican twist. Scott has a saying about Applebee's, god knows where he got it from, probably a Vince Vaughn movie. He says, 'Nobody goes to the Applebee's alone,' but little did he know it would be his own wife who would prove that theory wrong.

We ate our meals without too much conversation; we were all a little stunned, trying to process where we were and what we were doing there. I think I may have squeezed in a little margarita to lighten my mood. No sugar or syrup, because that wouldn't be healthy, right? We paid the bill, with a tip of course, then walked the streets of Portland trying to get our bearings.

We wandered around like zombies, not knowing what to do with ourselves because we were now wide awake. The only option was to go back to the hotel and watch TV.

Scott wasn't thrilled with all the ads and infomercials on American TV. Talk about whingeing, he turned it into a sport. But, we eventually went to sleep and woke up to a new day, albeit at 11.30am.

We fluffed about and then took ourselves off to a massive shopping centre we had noticed the night before. It was called the Lloyd Center and became affectionately known as the Lloydy, our home away from home.

On Saturday night we walked to a basketball game at the Rose Quarter, which was about six blocks from our hotel. Unlike the day before, the chill went through to our bones. It was absolutely freezing even with ski parkas, woollen scarves and boots. The Portland basketball team are called the Trail Blazers, so of course we supported them, our new home team. Scott and Remy had hotdogs, huge American-style ones with chilli, coleslaw, sauerkraut, relish, mustard and ketchup. I didn't indulge, of course, as white bread was a complete no-no. I watched enviously as they chowed down with no regard or compassion for me at all. Was I tempted, you ask? Yes I was, but my health apart from the bleeding obvious was good, very good, in fact, so I stuck religiously to the sugar-, gluten- and grain-free diet. The odd margarita or brandy was my guilty pleasure.

We managed to make it home without freezing to death. I made a beeline for the fireplace, put a log in and poked it around till the fire was raging. We sat around the fireplace listening to music. Scott and Remy were playing with their phones so I decided to write a letter to my mum.

Sunday arrived and it was more of the same, trying to keep warm and looking for another excuse to eat. I remember wanting that day to be over just as much as I wanted it to last as I knew the next morning I had my appointment at Providence Cancer Center to meet the people I had harassed for the past three months. I would be having my final tests to see if I qualified to take part in the study that would give me the best chance, the only chance as far as I was concerned, to save my life.

Chapter Nineteen

Letter to Mum in Heaven

Hi Mum,

Remember I told you we were trying to beg our way into a clinical trial in America? Well, after three months of begging and pleading we have finally been accepted and we are here in Portland, Oregon. It is not in the sticks, Mum, as we first thought, it is just above California, in the Pacific North West. It's bloody freezing, rainy and cold, just the way you like it.

Remy came with us, Mum, we just couldn't leave her. She is doing her Higher School Certificate, her last year at school and it tears me apart that my condition is going to get in the way of this. I will talk to her teachers and she will just have to get her work sent to us over here. She will graduate this year, Mum, if it's the last thing I do. I will make sure she does. It's not her fault this has happened to me and I won't let it get in the way of her future.

I had to say goodbye to Morgan on Friday and I think my heart, the one that was ripped out, is still on the front lawn in Sydney. Roxy has probably eaten it by now. And that's fine. There wasn't much left anyway. To leave Morgan like that was just cruel, cruel for all of us. She has Dad and Mark and the girls but she doesn't have us and in times like these you just want your mum. I know I do. I want you every day.

I have my first appointment with the doctor in the morning at 8am. It is the 3rd of March now and March, apparently, was when the chemotherapy would turn its back on me. Thank god I have some hope, Mum, and I'm hanging on to this hope with everything I've got.

Wish me luck, Mum, I need your love and support like never before. Tell Nanna I love her. Write back soon. Oh, and did you find Steve Jobs? Obviously not. Or maybe you did but you didn't understand a bloody word he said. I'm laughing out loud now. Love you, miss you.

Love Jule

Chapter Twenty

D-Day arrived, 4 March 2013, after a restless night. Guilt, fear, excitement, anxiety, visits from the monsters – the three of them were relentless all night long. *What if you don't qualify? What if they find a tumour on your brain? Maybe even two, you know how fast this thing can move. You can do this. No you can't. Yes you can.* My mind was messy.

I couldn't take it anymore so I got up and headed straight for the shower. It was still pitch black, 5.30am. I nearly washed all of my skin off. I thought I'd wash my hair to take up a bit of time, but then I remembered I didn't have any so that little time-wasting exercise wasn't going to work. By 6.30am I was dressed and ready. Blue jeans, white jumper and a yellow and blue silk scarf. I had to wear something bright, it was almost an obsession. My thick puffer jacket was waiting by the door. I would be sitting in front of the head doctor in one and a half hours' time.

I managed to fill in the next hour with three cups of tea in rapid succession while staring into the flames of the fire I'd lit, hoping to calm my mind. Then it was time to wake the other two, who clambered out of bed bleary-eyed. They robotically dressed themselves for the most important appointment of our lives.

It was freezing when we stepped outside, so we asked reception to order a cab for us. It arrived in minutes.

'Where are you folks going?' asked the driver.

'Providence Cancer Center,' I replied, finding it hard to believe the words that were coming out of my mouth.

'Sure,' he said, not even asking the address. I guessed he took a lot of folks to that place.

Five minutes in the cab and there it was, an eleven-storey building with those words in huge letters on the front. Providence Cancer Center.

Was this place going to be the answer to our prayers? God I hoped so. Would this place be worth leaving my daughter back home in Australia to deal with her fears? I'd eventually find out, but first there was a long, steep hill to climb.

We walked through the doors and over to the lifts on the right-hand side of the foyer. As usual Remy and I followed Scott – he takes charge in these situations and usually gets us where we need to be. He stopped at the black sign with the gold writing and pressed the button for level six. That was the floor marked with the words 'Clinical Trials'. The lift went straight to six, we walked out, turned right and followed the signs to the clinic door. By now my heart was racing.

Scott opened the door, ushered me in and we went straight up to the desk to check in. A beautiful woman with long, dark wavy hair looked up and said to us in her American drawl, 'Hey, you guys checkin' in?' I recognised that voice and looked down at her name tag. It was Patti, my new best friend who had delivered the good news six weeks earlier.

'Patti,' I said, 'it's Julie from Australia.'

'Jooollliiieee,' she said, then she came running around the desk and gave me a big hug. 'We have been looking forward to meeting you guys from Australia.'

With that I burst into tears and poor Patti felt awful. I regathered, trying to blame it on jet lag, but I don't think I was fooling anyone, including myself.

We took our seats and waited for my name to be called. By this stage I was tapping my foot, shaking my legs and squeezing Scott's hand as hard as I could. I think he even yelled *oowwee* at one stage, the big sook. I just didn't know what to do with myself, all the while trying to appear as calm as possible for Remy's sake.

After what seemed forever a door opened and a pretty nurse with ash-blonde hair stuck her head out and said, 'Julie Randall'. My heart did a complete backflip. I was about to meet these people. Doctor Walter Urba and Daniel Jackson, the people I had been harassing and pestering for so long. Scott got up with me; Remy stayed in the waiting room playing with her phone.

I didn't want her to hear all the gory details of my condition and I had learned the hard way that you can control a lot of things in life, but you can't control what other people say.

The nurse asked me to hop onto the scales. I nearly died when I saw the number '127' come up on the digital display window. Scott could see my concern and then, in a very patronising manner, said, 'That's pounds, you know, darl.'

I gave him a filthy look and just got on with following the almost military-style orders being barked at me, in a very nice way, by the check-in nurse. Put this under your tongue, put your arm out, give me your index finger, look into this light. I had done those tests so many times I had lost count. But this time I wanted to be the best. I wanted to be the healthiest cancer patient they had ever encountered. I had to show them I was as tough as nails and could handle anything they dished out to me. They had to put me in that trial. After all, I wasn't in Portland for a holiday!

The nurse seemed very happy with my results. She grabbed her clipboard, led us down the corridor and ushered us into a room to wait for the doctor. I was bordering on having an anxiety attack. It was like I was about to be interviewed to determine if my life was worth saving. Jiggling and shaking and cupping my hands, I was a nervous wreck.

Then there was a gentle knock on the door. 'Come in!' we said, feeling a little silly. There he was.

'Hello,' he said in a very welcoming manner. It wasn't Doctor Urba, it was Daniel Jackson. He looked like he was in his 30s and about five-foot-ten with a very slight build, dark hair, a moustache and goatee. He also wore thick-rimmed glasses. Very cool, very Portland, I was soon to find out. 'How are you folks doin'?' he asked, then shook Scott's hand and gave me a hug. Surprise, surprise, I burst into tears again. Daniel ignored the tears and started making small talk about our long flight. Scott answered all the questions, giving me time to compose myself. Then I gave him the biggest heartfelt thank you I had ever given anyone in my life. The man standing in front of us had worked tirelessly for me, a woman he didn't know, to overcome all of the objections and finally get the all-clear for us to come over.

Scott was asking a lot of questions about the trial and the results they were having with the drug. Daniel was positive but said he would love to get the number of responders up past 38 per cent. He then gave me a referral for CT and MRI scans, as we knew would be the case. The thought of an MRI sickened me for two reasons. I hate them, because of the claustrophobia thing, but worse than that, if I had any lesions on my brain I would be going back home, which was a notion too scary to take a position in my already overcrowded head.

Daniel finished his part of our pre-study meeting, said, 'See ya soon, folks!' and left the room. He had gone to get the head honcho, Doctor Walter Urba, the man who was instrumental in getting this immunotherapy trial off the ground. This guy was to become my second favourite man in the world.

A couple of minutes passed, then there was another little tap on the door. This time I just called out 'hiya' and in he walked. He looked about 60, was tall, around six-foot-two, with short salt-and-pepper hair and a golden complexion. Wow, what a striking man. He was super friendly, shaking hands with both of us, Scott's a little more firmly than mine. Something about him made us both fall in love with him immediately. He was it, he was the man. Like Daniel, he talked about the trial and the results they were achieving and reiterated that the drug doesn't work for everyone. He then congratulated us on our tenacity and determination to get ourselves over there and did what he called a routine examination, all the while chatting away, asking us about our family and our life in Australia, and was genuinely interested in the answers. Doctor Urba ended our session with, 'Well, folks, let's hope these scan results are all in your favour and we can get you on the drug ASAP.'

'Thank you, Doctor Urba, thank you so much,' I said as he left the room.

Scott and I walked down the hallway and into the reception room where Remy was waiting, playing on her phone, just as we'd left her. I had a slight spring in my step and was actually able to give her a genuine smile. We were all hungry, so we went down to the hospital cafeteria and had breakfast. I noticed that my breathing had become normal for the first time in as long as I could remember.

We went back to our new home, the Marriott Residence Inn, and crashed out. I was exhausted and I felt like I actually slept, another sensation I hadn't felt for a long time.

Trying to work out what to do with ourselves had already become an issue and we'd only been in Portland for three days. At that point the weather wasn't conducive to strolling around and taking in the sights, so the Lloyd Center it was. Because there is no sales tax in Oregon, everything seemed much cheaper. Our new favourite pastime became checking out the clothes, shoes and the jewellery and marvelling at how cheap they were compared with Australia. That afternoon, on Monday 4 March 2013, I bought a pinkie ring from Pandora. Made of silver hearts, it symbolised my friends and family who love me and also my strong will to stay alive for them; to respond to this treatment and find my way back home as soon as I possibly could. I missed them all so much already and the thought of Morgan so far away choked me up every time it crossed my mind. I have that ring on my pinkie finger right now. I rarely take it off.

We were lucky enough to have two baths in our hotel suite, so having a soak was another big time filler. That night I was in the bath when I noticed a lump on my left rib cage. *What the hell is that?* I thought. It certainly hadn't been there a week earlier. I called out to Scott to bring me the shampoo from the other bathroom but I really wanted a second opinion on what this thing was. He couldn't deny it, as much as he wanted to. A new tumour had formed. It was almost certain that going off the chemo had triggered the cancer again. I was devastated and scared but I had to hide it. Remy's anxiety had already gone to another level. She was having panic attacks and trouble sleeping. Being away from home and away from her friends in this strange, cold grey place had already started to take its toll on her. It broke my heart to see her like that. I certainly wasn't going to make it any worse by sharing this disturbing news.

Scott tried to comfort me by saying, 'That will be the last of it, darl, we are about to sort this out once and for all.' Thank god I had him there with me.

I was booked in for the scans early the next morning. It was cold and dark and I didn't want to wake Remy because she was sleeping so peacefully. I whispered to Scott that I would get a cab to the hospital and that he should stay with her. He reluctantly agreed. We were both so worried about her.

CT scans comprise a small scanner you go in and out of which only covers your chest, abdomen and pelvis, so I could handle it easily. You have to drink a revolting liquid that makes your body light up like a Christmas tree so the medicos can clearly see any tumours you may have lurking around. I got through it, ticked it off, it was done.

Then came the MRI with no Scott to rub my feet and comfort me with his loving, supportive words. If you haven't had an MRI scan, firstly, lucky you. They are much more intrusive than any of the others. You go into a tunnel with only the bottom of your legs sticking out. In my case they put a cage over my head and padding either side of my face, then to top it all off they supply headphones because the noise is deafening.

Try as I might to calm myself down, I couldn't. My anxiety was escalating. I sat in the cubicle with my white gown on, freaking out, and the more I told myself how important it was, the more uptight I became. My mind kept going back to the new lump I had found the night before and how crucial it was that I started this treatment pronto and responded to the drug. That only made it worse, though; it was all too much. The radiographer convinced me to lie on the bed and tried to talk me through it. I made three attempts at going into the scanner and each time I yelled for them to get me out. I couldn't do it. I was distraught and crying and all by myself. I had to get a cab back to the hotel and tell Scott what had happened. That day I was angry, angry at myself and the world, but I knew I had to keep going, just keep putting one foot in front of the other.

We went back the next day. I took medication and I took Scott, who rubbed my legs. Twenty minutes of hell, then it was over. I'd done it.

Chapter Twenty-one

Daniel had told us he wouldn't have the results for at least three days, and would call us when he did. The waiting was torture but there was absolutely nothing we could do about it. I couldn't sit around staring at the walls any longer so I suggested we go out for a drive. Scott reminded me that we didn't have a car. I think I was really losing it at that stage. Anyway, he suggested we hire one, so that's what we did.

Scott went down to the foyer and grabbed a few brochures. We didn't want to venture too far and Multnomah Falls seemed to fit the bill. It looked beautiful. I needed to get out into nature. I was missing yoga and Roxy and running in the park behind our house. I wanted to go to a spiritual place, re-focus my mind and sing my song. I was all out of sorts. I had to get back on track.

We hopped into the rental car and headed for the Columbia River Highway. Scott looked like he'd been driving on the other side of the road his whole life. I wouldn't have even contemplated driving that day, or any other day for that matter. I excused myself for not wanting to take on any more challenges at that particular point in my life.

Multnomah Falls is the second tallest year-round waterfall in America. We drove along the Columbia River for about 45 minutes, followed the signs and pulled into the carpark, looked up and there it was. One of the most stunning exhibits of nature I have ever seen. It was just divine. I could feel my spirit lift a little. We got out of the car, put on our parkas and walked across to the ticket office. You could hike up as far as the first bridge which was 69 feet (21 metres), or you could go all the way up to 540 feet (165 metres). We went right to the top. I remember that hike like it was yesterday – the noise of the water cascading down, through the rainforest and over the rocks covered with moss; my chest burning as we got higher and higher. I sang my song all the way up.

I am happy and healthy,
All my organs have healed,
My body and its organs have healed,
I have faith in life.

I started to feel connected to myself again, connected to my purpose and the reason I was there in Oregon. I had been knocked for six finding that new lump, but it was March and even if I had stayed in Australia and kept up the chemo, the doctor had told me it would stop working around that time. I had to push it to the back of my mind and keep my eye on the prize. That prize would be my life, the prize I had taken for granted for the past 50 years.

We climbed and we climbed and we climbed and eventually reached the top, where there was a little stream and a spectacular view below. It felt serene and peaceful. We made sure we took it all in.

Scott said he wanted to go a little higher – there was one more short climb you could do – and said he'd meet us at the bottom. He kept going and Remy and I started the long walk back down, which was not nearly as taxing as the way up but still a little daunting if you got too much speed up and lost your balance. It would be all over, red rover, and that would not have been a good thing for anyone, especially us. We didn't need to be paying thousands of dollars in airfares just to end up dead at the bottom of a cliff. Scott was waiting at the foot of the falls with a grin like a Cheshire cat. To this day, I don't know how he got down there so quickly and he refuses to let on. Supposedly there is only one way down that mountainside and he did not pass us. We would have seen him. It remains a mystery.

We had lunch at a restaurant which was elegant and quaint with a magical view of the falls. Scott had the clam chowder, which was to become a favourite for him. Remy and I had a Moroccan stew with salad on the side.

We drove back to our hotel a little more refreshed and alive than we had been that morning. It was a great feeling for all of us – we had managed the hike and given ourselves some much-needed endorphins.

A liver biopsy was the next thing on the agenda to complete the pre-trial qualifications. Believe it or not, I wasn't looking forward to that either, as I'd already had a biopsy to determine what form of cancer I had and it didn't tickle.

It was scary, painful and extremely distressing. The procedure was scheduled for 7am and we needed to be there by 6.30am. I had to drag the others out of bed this time as Scott was driving me to the hospital. We left around 6.10am and I asked him if he knew how to get there. 'Yes,' he said, sounding very confident, so I didn't give it a second thought until he started sounding a little frustrated. To cut a long story short, we got lost, very lost, and had to call a taxi so we could follow it to the hospital. We were a little late but the painful biopsy was performed and I lived through it. We were ticking the boxes one by one.

Waiting for the results of these tests was horrible, as always, and the mean monster was having a field day. *What if you have another tumour on your brain? Maybe even two or three? They won't take you. You realise that, don't you? What if something's wrong with your blood tests? They won't want you then, will they? They'll just send you home. And then what?*

Please stop, I told him. *Can you just let me live in the moment? Get out of my head.* I needed to try to occupy myself with something else.

Scott loves to surf, swim, paddle, anything to do with the ocean and as you know he calls it his religion, his church, so I was thinking a little churchiness couldn't go astray. I got online and revisited the coastal town I had briefly researched before we left. It looked like a cool place and it was only a 90-minute drive.

Cannon Beach is a picturesque little town on the northwest coastline of Oregon and soon became one of our favourite places on earth. It is famous for a lot of things, including its coastline with panoramic views; its rainbow-like sunsets when the clouds stay away, of course; Haystack Rock; and its funky art galleries and cafés.

I booked a room then we threw a few things into our overnight bags and hit the road, this time printing out a map so there would be no taxi escorts required. We drove through the city following all the directions to the coast. It was grey for a change, but we were growing used to that. About an hour into the drive the scenery changed, with huge bottle-green spruce trees lining either side of the road. I may have even lasted three minutes without thinking about trying to save my life. The results of my tests were due that afternoon. The thought made my stomach flip. I had waited for results many times since that fateful day at work, but these were even more crucial than any before.

Arriving in Cannon Beach was special. It was so different from any place I had ever been. The houses were mostly little cottages, very beach-housey but in an old-fashioned way, with a slight Dutch influence. The town centre was cute and welcoming, with beautiful bright-pink flowers on windowsills and in pots on the footpath. There were boutique wine shops and lovely restaurants. It made me smile and I certainly wasn't doing enough of that at the time.

The three of us were hungry so we decided to have lunch before checking in to our hotel. We found a carpark, so that's where we stopped. It was right outside the Driftwood Restaurant and Lounge and the menu looked all right, so we went in and found a cosy atmosphere and tables with red and white checked tablecloths. I can even remember what I ordered. A Driftwood Burger without the bun – meat, cheese and pickle with an amazing sauce. Scott had clam chowder and Remy a burger with the bun.

We jumped back into the car and went to check in to our hotel, which was okay but in hindsight a little too far out of town. I had just carried my bag into the room when I heard our local American phone ring; it was in Scott's pocket. We knew who it was because no one else knew the number. I felt sick as I always did when expecting one of these calls.

'Hello,' Scott said and then, 'Yes mate, I'll put her on.' So this was it. All the tests had been done. Daniel Jackson had the final decision and he was about to tell me what it was.

'Hi Daniel,' I said nervously, walking out onto the verandah away from the others.

'Well, we have all the tests back, annnnndddddddd . . .' (which seemed to go on forever) '. . . your brain is clear and we think you have plenty to work with. We biopsied one of your three liver tumours and got the information we needed. We will start you on the drug on Monday.'

'Thanks Daniel,' I said, 'that's wonderful news.' Then I hung up the phone and went straight into the bathroom and cried. I cried tears of happiness followed by tears of sorrow. On my last scan in Australia there was only one tumour in my liver. The chemotherapy had banished two of them. Now they were back, along with the new one on my rib cage. This thing had returned and with a vengeance, it seemed.

This treatment had to work, and fast.

Chapter Twenty-two

I can only describe my feelings at that time as a combination of elation and fear, a rare mix of emotions that took on a life of their own. I was elated that our determination and persistence had paid off, and deeply fearful that if it didn't work my life was virtually over.

Scott and Remy were relieved, but by that stage we had become a little jaded. Although it was actually the first time we all had an inkling that this mission *not impossible* wasn't a big, disastrous, expensive mistake.

I wished Daniel hadn't mentioned the liver tumours. But he had, so what could I do? If I'd thought the chemo was going to protect me forever, I wouldn't have been in Oregon in the first place. It was a hard pill to swallow but it was the truth and I had no choice but to accept it. We still had hope, and that's all we could ask for.

The ocean, or the 'seaside', as they call it, was just across the road from our cottage so we decided to rug up and go for a long walk on the beach. It wasn't like the beaches we were used to in Australia, but it was a beach nonetheless. It was cold and windy and reminded me of a beach you would see in Ireland rather than the west coast of America. Scott pointed out that it was the same ocean we swam in at home. It was the Pacific and if I dived in and swam for about ten years I would be back home with Morgan. I was missing her so much already and we had only been gone just over a week. I missed Roxy too and she'd be missing me and wondering where on earth we all were. I found it hard to look at people playing with their dogs on the beach.

The sand was dark grey and pebbly and it was a packed lunch and a camel ride from where the sand starts to the shore. Probably like a three-minute walk, not easy in Ugg boots!

There were people everywhere building sandcastles and throwing frisbees but not in their swimmers; they were dressed in their winter woollies. It was such a funny sight. You would never see that in Australia. One little boy was swimming in the ocean having a lovely time, with his mum standing at the shore wearing a woollen coat, knee-high boots and a beanie. The water temperature was, well, freezing, let's put it that way. It was hilarious.

Some of the people were riding along the shore on these odd little three-wheel tricycles, which looked like a lot of fun. We kept walking up the beach all the way to Haystack Rock, a huge rock sticking out of the ocean surrounded by lots of other smaller ones. It was spectacular.

I pretended to be cheery that afternoon but I was having lots of morbid feelings. I knew for sure that I couldn't keep myself alive with diet, yoga, exercise and meditation on their own. That had become a fact. But I did know deep down in my soul that those practices were keeping me healthy, fit and strong, and being that way would give my body the best chance of the immunotherapy drug doing what it is designed to do.

The next morning after a short session of yoga and meditation we decided to explore the town from one end to the other. The skies were grey as usual, but we left the car behind and off we went, this time replacing the Ugg boots with trainers.

The town centre is divine. It is an arty place and everything reflects that – the street flowers, the colours, the architecture. I wasn't surprised to discover Cannon Beach is often listed as one of the world's top 100 beautiful places.

We found a gallery café and had lunch, then wandered a little more. All of a sudden it became apparent that most of the grown-ups were strolling around with plastic long-stemmed wine glasses in their hands, sipping away. It looked like a lot of fun. Scott could see my enthusiasm but gently reminded me with a little hint of sarcasm, 'What a shame you don't drink wine anymore, darl.' It turned out it was the weekend of the 'Savor Cannon Beach Wine Walk'. Everyone roams around from shop to shop tasting wines from the local regions. It was an amazing atmosphere. I wished I was there under different circumstances but the truth was if I wasn't under those circumstances, I wouldn't have been there at all. I'd barely even heard of Oregon, let alone Cannon Beach.

On the Sunday afternoon of that weekend we drove back to Portland to get ready to start my treatment. It was finally going to happen. I was going to receive this drug intravenously the next day. I didn't speak much out loud on the way home but I did have a hell of a lot to say to my insides.

I talked to it like a coach would talk to a team the day before an Olympic final. 'Come on, you know you can do this! This is your chance to shine. You will be getting a drug that is going to kick your immune system right back into action and help it to repair all of its cells.' I asked my body to welcome the drug, make friends with it and please let it do what it was there to do: get us back on track. I asked my mind to be strong and focused and through meditation I visualised the drug going through my system and repairing my cells. I made the most of the 90-minute trip back to Portland – non-stop pep talks with myself from door to door.

The next morning we were up early to get to the Cancer Center by 8am. I would be the first there and the last to leave. I put on blue jeans, a grey fluffy cardigan and a hot-pink tie-dye scarf.

The trial I had signed up for is called a biomarker trial, which means they would take blood for testing, then give me the drug and take bloods all day every hour so that the scientists could see what the drug was doing in my system. That was the deal, it was an experiment.

I checked in again with my new bestie, Patti, then went through all the routine stuff, weight, blood pressure, then they led us into the clinic. It was L-shaped with a nurses' station in the middle and all the usual recliner chairs along the back walls with plenty of space in between and windows to let in natural light. It was white and sterile like most hospitals, but it had a nice feel. It just felt right. The nurses all jumped up when we walked in, genuinely excited to see their new friends from Australia. I became extremely fond of those nurses. I will never forget them as long as I live.

One of the nurses, Catherine, led me over to a chair with a big sign on it saying 'reserved for research'. It came over me like a wave that I was just about to take part in a science project, but I do remember thinking that at least it didn't say 'reserved for that pain-in-the-arse serial pest from Australia'.

There was no mucking around. I sat down and Catherine came over with her trolley. Before I knew it she had accessed my portacath and blood was pouring through the tube. She must have drawn ten vials of blood. She finished labelling them, took them away, then walked back over to us with a big plastic bag about three-quarters full with a clear liquid substance in it. She asked me my name and my date of birth. I responded 'Julie Ann Randall eight-six-sixty-two.' She looked a little perplexed. 'Oh,' I said, 'six-eight-sixty-two,' after twigging that Americans put the month before the day. She seemed happy enough with that and showed me the bag. I didn't really notice anything else except for the PD-1 that was in a bolder typeface than anything else. I smiled at her and said, 'Yep, let's go!' and she connected the drug – which would later be known as Nivolumab – to my tube. We were off on this new journey of hope.

Chapter Twenty-three

It was quite the marathon that first day in the chair, nine solid hours in fact. I sent Scott and Remy back home as soon as I was connected up. I saw no point in them sitting next to me all day with all the carry-on. There were a lot of other patients in the room, and I decided my teenage daughter didn't need to witness that.

I did feel like a lab rat by the end of it, but that's what I'd signed up for. This was research. It wasn't all about me. I was just a number. I would become known to the scientists as Patient 71. It turned out that the trial should have been cut off at 70 patients, but because of all our begging and pleading, they decided to make room for one more. I'm not sure if it was the emotional blackmail, the Hippocratic Oath reminder, the doctor in Newcastle or the offer of surf lessons in Australia, but something had struck a chord that became, for me, the difference between life and death. And for the first time in my life I was happy to be 'just a number'.

In the clinic that day I met a beautiful young girl, Jenny, who volunteered on her days off from university. She would walk around to all the patients and make sure they were warm and bring them tea and biscuits. What a delightful, giving human being. She wasn't hanging out with her friends or shopping up a storm or even studying or doing assignments. She was devoting her time to people, people she felt needed to be as comfortable as possible while receiving treatment for this unwanted guest trying to infiltrate and destroy their existence. Jenny looked after me all day. We chatted about anything and everything while she supplied me with copious amounts of tea. No biscuits, of course. Scott had made me a chicken salad so I wasn't starving.

Jenny was the perfect distraction and time filler. That afternoon I had nodded off in my chair while she was looking after other patients. I woke up to a note on my tray table. 'Hi Julie, I have gone home. I didn't want to wake you up. You looked so beautiful and peaceful asleep in the chair.' The sun peeped through the clouds and shone through the window just as I awoke to that message. I felt like something special had happened, but it would be six long weeks before I would find out.

I was in the study. *They can't stop me now*, I thought. I really wished Morgan and my father and my brother and sisters were there with me. I wanted my mum. I loved and missed her so much. I missed my friends. I couldn't believe it had only been a week and a half; it felt like six months. The mean monster kept reminding me that I would be there for two years and asking me, *How the hell will you deal with that?* I told him I was becoming awake to him and I knew what he was up to. I knew he was trying to derail me and throw me off the path because it was all too hard. I knew he was trying to protect me from disappointment. *I get where you're coming from*, I told him, *but I have to take one day at a time and I'd really like it if you and I could get on the same page. If I'd listened to you I wouldn't have come to Portland at all.*

And at that moment, it dawned on me that my childhood Odyssey of having conversations with characters in my head had returned to help me cope with all the conflicting crazy thoughts and scenarios constantly running through my mind. I realised my little game had made a comeback so I had others to talk to and keep me grounded so I didn't lose the plot completely. The monsters were there to help save my life. Suddenly it all made sense.

I had to go to the hospital every day for the first week to have my bloods taken and analysed, and apart from what was going on in the science labs, which I had no idea about, my regular blood counts were all good. I did feel a few flu-like symptoms for a couple of days which was nothing really, and after that I was as good as gold. It was a little unnerving as I thought I should be feeling sick and revolting, but I didn't. I was running on the treadmill in the hotel, singing my song and going on long walks with Scott and Remy.

After that first week I would only have an infusion of PD-1 every fortnight and go in for a check-up each week. It felt bizarre being so far away from home trying to occupy our time when it would only end up being around five hours a fortnight that I spent at the hospital.

One morning a couple of days after my first infusion I was having a shower when I ran my hand over the area where I had noticed the scary lump about a week earlier. I kept feeling and feeling, and there was nothing there. I called out to Scott to come into the bathroom. I motioned to him to put his hand on the spot. He put two fingers together and moved them around. He looked up at me and said, 'It's gone.'

I said, 'Really? I'm not just imagining this, am I?'

He said, 'It's gone,' with a big smile on his face.

I knew it was just something little but I prayed it meant something big. I didn't want to get overexcited but I couldn't help it. I also knew that this treatment sometimes only had a partial response, meaning it worked on some tumours and not others, but, hey, I was running with this one. You bloody bet I was. I needed to believe. I stayed in the shower talking to myself for the next fifteen minutes, thanking my cells, my mind and my body. *Come on*, I was saying, *we can do this!*

The nice monster joined in. *Look at you go, girl, look how far you've come!*

Yes, twelve thousand kilometres, I said and we had a little giggle. I knew it was more about my vital organs, but this must mean something, surely?

We got through the next week or so the best we could, then Remy started to make noises about going home to Australia. I had been in constant contact with her teachers on email and they had been sending us schoolwork – I was still determined to get her through that final year of school, no matter what. She wanted Scott to go home with her but I didn't want to part with him. It became a bone of contention. I couldn't bear the thought of being in that cold, dark city alone. The sun had not returned after showing itself for five minutes in the clinic on that first afternoon of my treatment. After much discussion, we agreed that Scott would fly down to LA from Portland, put Remy on a flight to Australia, where my friend Liz would meet her at the airport. I had spoken with my sisters, my buddies, my dad and of course Morgan and asked them to take care of her. It ripped my heart out that she would be leaving and going all the way home without either of us with her in such a fragile state. But it would mean she could go back to school and be with her friends and Morgan, and maybe start to feel a little human again. I ended up telling her about the lump that had disappeared after the treatment. I didn't want to get her hopes up just in case things didn't turn out as planned, but I also thought knowing about it might help her rest a little easier.

Scott booked the flights and far too soon the day came when my baby girl was leaving me and going home by herself. Scott would put her on the 10.35pm flight, stay in LA for the night, then return to Portland the next day. While we were packing her bags I had a lump in my throat as big as a pineapple. I was telling her how much I loved her, how we were going to get through this and things would be back to normal before we knew it. I would find a way to come home. I reiterated the importance of her going back to school and finishing her final year, and reminded her that she would have lots of people around her. She nodded and hugged me tightly, then it was time for them to leave. While I said goodbye I managed to keep my cool, but when they left I collapsed behind the door and cried and cried and cried. I didn't want her to go. I didn't want to be without her and I didn't know when I would see her again. I didn't want Scott to be gone for a minute, let alone two whole days.

The elation of the lump disappearing went right out the window and the negativity started to creep back in. It was a cold and miserable day and I didn't know what to do with myself. I didn't want to leave the room but I didn't want to stay inside. I remembered that one of the nurses had given me a card for a grief counsellor named Christa who worked at the hospital in case any of us needed someone to talk to.

I found the card and called the number. I needed to try to get some sort of relief from the complete despair I was going through. I left a message and I must have sounded desperate as she called me back five minutes later. She was so caring, but what could she say? What could anyone say? I had one daughter at home in Australia and the other one on her way; I had advanced cancer and neither she nor anyone else could guarantee this treatment would work *and* she certainly couldn't tell me when I would hold my children again. That thought was burning me from the inside out. Christa listened and empathised with me with all her heart but that's all she could do.

I walked around in circles that day, my mind jumping from one thing to another. I tried meditating, I tried doing yoga, but nothing was working. I was a complete mess. I didn't even stop crying when the room attendant came in to clean the room. I thought about saying 'no thanks' when she knocked, but I felt so lonely that even the presence of the Hispanic non-English-speaking maid was a bonus. Finally I succumbed to lighting the fire even though it was only midday. What a saviour that was. I had it going all day. I kept ringing down to reception for more fire logs and didn't leave the room.

When it was a reasonable time in Australia I started to call my sisters, my dad and my friends on Viber (a mobile calling and texting app), crying in their ears and expressing my grief. They all listened and hugged me through the phone and I could feel they were hurting for me, just as much as I was hurting myself. I couldn't have survived that day without them. Some of them would have been at work but they didn't let on. They would have lost their jobs before they cut me short. I love each and every one of them for listening to me that day.

While I was on one of my reach-out Viber calls, the local US phone rang. It was Scott and I didn't want to hear that she'd gone. I did not want him to say the words. He didn't, as it turned out. He had put her on the plane and went to the bar for a drink when his phone rang. It was Remy, she couldn't do it. She'd boarded the plane, sat in her seat, then started to freak out. She told one of the flight attendants she couldn't stay onboard. It was a bittersweet moment. Bitter for her but sweet for me. She'd really wanted to go back home. The poor little darling had been dragged into a nightmare. They *both* stayed in LA that night and *both* returned the next day. I loved being able to hug her again, but it would only be for another seven days. Scott booked flights for the next week. They were *both* going back home to Australia.

Well, if you thought I sounded distraught in the previous few paragraphs, that was nothing. The following week I would say goodbye to both of them. Remy needed to get home and she couldn't do it on her own. Somehow, deep down inside me, I had to find the strength to let them go. It would be the best thing for Scott and the girls to be home together. Every time I thought about it I felt like throwing up. How the hell would I cope? Staying in the moment at that time was almost impossible. I would try not to cry in front of Remy but when she was in the shower I would let loose on Scott. I really am surprised that my husband has one ounce of sanity left.

The countdown was on; there were four days to go. I was on my favourite chair in my favourite position in front of the fire while the other two were watching TV. I had told my family and friends that they would both be going home and tried to be brave, but I wasn't fooling anyone.

My phone rang, it was a Viber call from one of my best friends, Deb. Without hesitation she said, 'I'm coming over. I arrive at 12.15 on the 28th of March.' It was the exact day Remy and Scott would be leaving to go home to Australia. I couldn't believe it. I wasn't going to be alone. I couldn't speak. I was so happy. And grateful – she wasn't rolling in money and she had a really busy life. My family would be gone, but I would have my friend with me, just for a week, but at the time it meant the world.

Chapter Twenty-four

The next four days were beyond hard. We coped by walking around the city and stocking up on tax-free T-shirts for Remy. The thought of both of them leaving was unimaginable, even with the news that Deb would be arriving on the same day.

I had spent very little time away from Scott since my diagnosis and could only cope when he was by my side. I didn't want to say goodbye to him. I just didn't know how I was going to do that.

All too soon it was 28 March 2013 and it was time to say goodbye to my people. Remy had packed her bags again and Scott had to do the same. We went down to the foyer and called a taxi to the airport. As usual it came right away and we were on the highway heading out of town.

The airport came into view way too quickly. Scott and Remy checked in their bags and I wished like hell that I was checking in mine. My head was foggy and if it hadn't been midday I would have thrown down a couple of drinks, which would have probably made things worse. Their flight was called and we moved towards the departure gates. I was completely devastated saying goodbye. I kept hugging and hugging them and wouldn't let them go, but they had to go. I was a mess.

At exactly the moment that I knew I couldn't hold on any longer, Scott looked up and smiled at someone behind me. It was Deb. An angel had arrived just when I needed one the most. I hugged and kissed Scott and Remy for the last time and watched them make their way through the gates. Deb put her arm around me, grabbed me so tightly almost in a headlock so I couldn't turn around and led me away. I knew I had a life-threatening disease but it felt more like I was going to die of a broken heart. The only thought that nearly comforted me was the fact that they would be home with Morgan.

Deb had been one of the first to find out about my seizure all those months back, because I had planned to go to her place after work that day for a catch-up on my way home. She has been my friend for about 25 years. She is pretty and smart. We play touch football together and have shared so many fun times.

She was devastated when she found out what had happened to me that Thursday. Her son Patrick said it's the only time he has ever seen her cry. What an amazing friend and she still thinks I don't know it was her who dropped the $500 cash into our letterbox to help us with medical bills. I saw her from my bedroom window.

I really don't know how I would have coped if she wasn't at the airport that day. She reminded me I was there for a reason and a pretty bloody good one at that.

The uncertainty of it all, however, was like being in a pitch-black tunnel trying to find your way out into the light. It was now time to dig deep and toughen up. Deb had left her family and travelled all the way across the Pacific to be with me so I wasn't alone. I had to make her experience as enjoyable as possible.

I pulled myself together and focused on her. We went back to the hotel, dropped off her bags and got ourselves out and about – she wanted to stay awake to get in sync with Portland time. We started off at the Lloydy, of course. It was fun showing her all the shops and the bargains then having a late lunch and catching up. There was only one place I could eat at the Lloyd Center as it wasn't easy to get takeaway food while on a paleo style of diet. It was a Lebanese takeaway shop and I ordered the same thing every time: special chicken with hommus, olives, cucumber and tomato. The owner's sons, Muhammad and Bilail, became my friends and started preparing my meal as soon as they saw me approaching. When I found myself in Portland alone I would go to the Lloydy just to chat with them. I would wait patiently while they served customers in between our conversations. They promised me they would visit me in Australia one day.

Deb and I caught up on all the home gossip, chatting about anything and everything. A huge piece of my heart did go back to Australia that day but another piece of my heart had arrived to be by my side.

That night we actually went to a sports bar, which was a first – we hadn't been to any bars beforehand as Remy wasn't 21. We ordered a couple of margaritas and I shared what I had learned about Portland so far. Then we went home and got cosy in front of the fire.

I was still sporting the hairpiece but I had started to sprout some little white spikes all over my head. The new hair was like down, like a baby chicken, but it was there and it was comforting to know it was making a comeback. By then I had been off the chemo for more than two months and the immune therapy drug does not cause hair loss, an added bonus. I told Deb about it and she asked if she could have a squizz. Feeling a little relaxed after the margarita I agreed. I'll never forget that night. Deb said, 'You look great, I love it.' I trusted her. I knew she really meant what she said, so from that moment on I did not put the hairpiece back on my head. I was overseas, I knew very few people, so I thought I might as well rock it.

The following morning at around 9am my local phone rang. It was one of the nurses from the Cancer Center, asking if I had time to go to the hospital. They had a young girl, a patient in the clinic, who was refusing to have treatment. She had a form of lymphoma and was very sick. They had told her they had a patient from Australia in a clinical trial for melanoma. I guess it was just to make conversation, hoping to bring her around to the idea of having the treatment which made her feel very sick and extremely nauseous.

Apparently she was obsessed with Australia and when the nurses were talking about me, it seemed to change her demeanour. 'Of course I'll come, I'll be there in half an hour,' I told them. Deb understood and I called a cab right away.

Rebecca was 21. She was there with her mother who looked drained. Rebecca had been undergoing treatment for a long time and was little and frail with no hair on her head, no eyelashes and no eyebrows. She was very cranky and negative about everything. We chatted about me, my condition and Australia. The kangaroos and koalas, the beaches and the lifestyle and I explained to her why I was there. She had always dreamed of going to Australia so I told her she had a place to stay. She finally agreed to get her treatment. I stayed and talked to her and her mum for the full two hours of her infusion. I haven't seen Rebecca since and I often think of her and hope she made it through.

The next time I went to the clinic I gave the nurses my hair-piece to send to her as they told me she couldn't afford a wig. I felt great about helping her that day and focusing on someone apart from myself. There were so many people walking in my shoes; it is cruel, unbelievably cruel, and only we, the people walking in those shoes, can totally understand.

Deb and I went to Multnomah Falls and I enjoyed it just as much as the first time. We also took a trip to Mount Hood, which is a picturesque mountain you can see from miles around when the weather is fine. It looks surreal, like it has been dropped into the landscape of a scene from a Hollywood movie. It's around 3500 metres and is the only resort in North

America to have skiing all year round. It was freezing but finally we had sunshine – it made such a difference to see the sun and I couldn't wait to tell Scott and Remy who were convinced it was never going to make an appearance. That week went fast. I had been dreading this moment. It was time for Deb to go home.

Chapter Twenty-five

I had been trying so hard to be mindful and not obsess about being alone. Deb had to go. She had to go back to her family and her work. There was no way of getting around that. I was trying to hold it all together as I didn't want her to leave feeling bad when she had done such a wonderful, selfless thing for me.

She was packing up her things and realised there was no way she was going to fit all her extra purchases into her suitcase, so we had to have another little trip over to the Lloydy. The whole time I had an ache in my stomach and a feeling of loneliness I had never experienced before. It was a double whammy. The lonely big hole I felt from having a life-threatening illness that no one could fill – not Scott, not Remy or Morgan, no one. And the physical loneliness I was already experiencing knowing that in three hours' time I would be completely and utterly by myself.

Deb found the perfect solution to her over-shopping issue in a black and white zebra-print carry-on that cost next to nothing. We went back home (my hotel home) and we finished her packing. She was almost done and then there was a knock on the door. I thought it was housekeeping and I was a little bummed, as I wanted them later when I needed company.

I walked to the door and opened it. I could not believe my eyes, it was my sister Kerri and my sister-in-law Jenny. My mouth fell open like a clown at a circus, then I burst into tears and hugged them both so tightly. Everyone was crying. My big brother, Mark, had paid for them to come over so I wasn't left alone and they'd decided to make it a surprise. Deb was in on it and helped them work out the timing so I didn't have to be by myself for one minute. I kept looking at them, saying, 'I can't believe you guys are here!' How lucky I am to have such amazing, devoted family and friends. What a gift it was to have Kerri and Jenny with me, and they were staying for ten whole days. When my big sister was with me I felt closer to my mum.

It was still sad to say goodbye to Deb. I didn't like saying goodbye to anyone at that time. The mean monster always told me that I may never see that person again. Thank goodness Kerri and Jenny were with me that day, for which I thanked the universe over and over again.

I was now becoming a tour guide and of course the first stop was the Lloydy after explaining the no-tax-in-Oregon thing and showing them all the bargains. The Australian dollar was at parity with the US dollar at that time which made shopping even sweeter.

Unfortunately the next day it was time for me to go back to the hospital – I had to have another liver biopsy as part of the study. I didn't want them to get up too early so I got myself to the hospital and they would come and pick me up.

I wasn't thrilled about having the biopsy and I didn't want to experience the pain from the previous two procedures, so I asked for more drugs. Not very pleasant at all having a large needle pushed through your chest and into your liver. I recall being rather out of it, but I do remember Doctor Urba and Daniel Jackson pointing at the screen and talking about what they were seeing. I was waiting for one of them to say, 'It's all gone. There's nothing to see here.' But they didn't, so I didn't ask. I didn't want to hear anything negative and decided to adopt the no-news-is-good-news philosophy.

Kerri and Jenny were in the foyer waiting for me. I felt revolting and nauseous and it dawned on me how horrible it would have been if I'd been on my own. They helped me into a cab and I started to feel sicker and sicker. I was going to throw up and there was just no stopping it. When the taxi stopped at some traffic lights I opened the door and just vomited my heart out. For the first time I felt happy to be in that strange city where no one I knew could possibly be witnessing that event.

Kerri and Jenny waited on me hand and foot. I did not get out of bed until the next morning and 24 hours later I was back to my old self. Then I had to return for the treatment. Dragging other people into that environment wasn't ideal, as there were some really sick patients in the clinic looking yellow and frail. But I was so grateful to have them by my side.

Two weeks had passed since I had seen my husband and I missed him so much it actually hurt. I missed Morgan and Remy and used to sit in front of the fire, close my eyes and imagine I was home with them all on the sofa with Roxy curled up at my feet. Roxy would be missing me so much. She would be missing our runs in the park and chasing the rabbits. I knew there was no way Scott and the girls would have time to do all those things with her.

I couldn't bring myself to Skype my family. I couldn't handle it. I would just break down and start weeping, which would not be good for anyone, so I stuck to calling them on Viber. That was another blessing. Viber. I would still be paying off the phone bill if it wasn't for that service.

Three days to go before my roommates were going home and Scott had told me very gently there were no more surprises in the wings. No one was coming to tag the girls. That notion was unbearable.

We decided it would be nice to go down to Cannon Beach to spend the remainder of their stay. I had told them how much I loved it, so they were keen to go and check it out. I ordered a driver, which would have been an expensive exercise, but between the three of us it worked out okay.

It was April and it was freezing. The girls loved Cannon Beach and it was fun exploring the bars. We spent a whole day in a bar called the Cannon Beach Hardware and Public House, or more colloquially, the Brew and Screw. It is a hardware store and a bar all in one place. Just a classic. They had the best bloody marys and oyster shooters we had ever tasted. We had a couple of bloody marys that day, I was allowed to have them occasionally as long as there was no sugar. I was going to have fun with the girls no matter what. After all, it was essential that I felt joy. Bill the Biologist had said so! There were some interesting, vibey people there and we laughed all day long. I felt good; I was doing my very best to stay present.

We returned to Portland and, like Deb, they both needed an extra bag to cart home their purchases. Then that horrible time came when I had to say goodbye to my beautiful sister and sister-in-law. It was time for them to go home. Scott had broken it to me: there was no one else coming. This time I had to face my scary world alone. This time it would really happen.

Chapter Twenty-six

Keep it together, Julie; please, please dig deep, I kept telling myself as the girls zipped up their bags and checked they had their travel documents. I had to say goodbye and unless my husband was playing a nasty joke, there would be no one from Australia knocking on the door any time soon. I had been trying to plan what to do to keep my sanity and pass the time after the girls had gone and the only thing I could come up with was to go walking and running in between trips to the shopping centre, which by then was losing its appeal.

Their taxi arrived and I helped them carry their bags down the stairs. We were all crying and they both hugged me tightly. Goodbye was my least favourite word and I seemed to be saying it constantly. The tears were flowing freely as I waved them goodbye. The feeling I felt that day is hard to put into words.

'Gutted' comes to mind, but that doesn't begin to give it justice. Hollow, coupled with devastation, fear, anger, loneliness, heartbreak and terror might come a bit closer. I was alone halfway around the world in a strange place receiving an experimental drug for a life-threatening illness. It doesn't get much worse than that. I wanted Scott so badly at that moment and I couldn't even talk to him as it was the middle of the night at home.

Being semi-prepared for that moment, I had dressed in tights, running shoes and a hoodie. I had to try to focus and dig down deep. I ran around and around the block that day, about ten times. I didn't want to go too far from home base. I sang my song out loud and I didn't care who heard me.

I am happy and healthy,
All my organs have healed,
My body and its organs have healed,
I have faith in life.

I must have walked and run for two hours and absolutely exhausted myself, which was the plan. All I wanted was to hear my husband's voice. I needed to listen to one of his pep talks but that would have to wait. I walked over to see Muhammad and Bilail. I needed to force some food down. I was getting skinnier and skinnier, but not in a good way. It was my diet coupled with heartbreak and stress. I needed to stay strong; I didn't want to waste away.

I managed to get through the next few hours before I called home. I spoke to my girls and when they put the phone up to

Roxy's ear they said she was doing that funny thing dogs do when they tilt their heads to one side. I was imagining that face and it made me smile. Scott came on the phone. I choked back the tears.

We talked for an hour; I didn't want to hang up. He said he was trying to get all of his work sorted out so he could come back over as soon as possible. Even a day seemed too long. I wanted them all with me. God it hurt like hell. I finally let him go and just stared into the fire. I don't know how much time passed. I didn't eat any dinner and ended up falling asleep in my chair.

The next morning my doctor called, asking if I would like to get involved in a fundraising project and, if so, did I have time to go in and discuss it with them. After consulting with my very open diary, I enthusiastically agreed. I didn't have a car and cabs were expensive, so I decided I would walk. I had driven the route so many times and it only took about seven minutes, so surely walking couldn't be that hard. It took me about an hour but I found my way.

Doctor Urba introduced me to a woman named Shari Scales, one of the most beautiful, angelic people I have ever met in my life. Shari talked about a couple of projects. One was to raise money for research at Providence and the other was to raise money to build new guest housing. Providence offered affordable housing, but it was very old, very basic and to me very depressing. We had looked at it originally when we first arrived in Portland, but we just wouldn't have coped there. Remy was with us and she was suffering from anxiety. She was going through enough, she didn't need to be away from home in awful living conditions. The room that was available to us was on a busy highway and basically underground. My dad wanted us to be comfortable so he paid for us to stay at the Marriott. I could not have imagined being in that accommodation under those circumstances, but that was all about to change.

I happily agreed to become involved in these projects, which would mean being interviewed and making videos for the Providence website. I had promised in my quest to get into the trial that I would volunteer and help in any way I could. I'd meant it and I would keep my promise no matter what. I felt a little better when I left the hospital that day. Feeling like you're useful can be so uplifting. I'd spent far too long being focused on myself. I had to stay in my lane when it came to healing, but I decided there was also some room for helping others.

Shari wanted both Scott and me to do the videos. He was excited when I told him on the phone that day; we were both passionate about giving back. He also told me he had booked his ticket to come back in fourteen days' time. He seemed disappointed that I didn't sound excited, but I explained to him that fourteen days without him felt like fourteen years.

I counted down the sleeps and got through each day with a combination of exercise, treatment, yoga, meditation and journalling by the fire. On the last night before he was due back, I can never remember being so excited and looking forward to anything so much in my life. He was due to arrive at 12pm the next day and I had planned to catch a train to the airport to meet him. I got up early and went over to the Lloydy. He hadn't seen me with my spiky short hair and I was determined to look as pretty as possible. I couldn't put my hairpiece on, that ship had sailed, and he is a long-hair type of guy. I bought a hot-pink leather jacket that was on sale, well that's what I told him, and some big earrings from GAP, went home and dolled myself up. Then it was time to go, so I walked to the station and jumped on the train. I felt elated and nervous and excited; I couldn't wait to be back in his arms. I made my way to the arrivals gate and waited. Lots of people were flooding through and it was about five minutes before I saw him and when I did my heart skipped a beat. He drew closer and closer and he had a huge grin on his face. We both started crying and hugged each other. He pulled back, looked at me and said, 'Pinky Tuscadero, I like it!' The leather jacket and the short spiky hair reminded him of Suzi Quatro. God love him. We went home, we made love. He slept and I lay next to him feeling at peace, a feeling that was often very hard to come by at that time. It was bliss that he was right there beside me.

Nothing had been said, but I knew Scott had made sure he was back for my scans. In six days I would have the scans that would ultimately map my future. I felt good physically but I had felt good when I fell to the ground with a brain seizure, so I knew all too well that unfortunately that was no indication of what was happening on the inside.

We decided to go down to Cannon Beach to get our minds off things and as always it didn't disappoint. This time we had sunshine, laughter *and* fun. The scans were always there and the monsters argued with each other from time to time but I tried to stay out of it. I had worked out how to enjoy myself anyway.

Scott saw a sign for live music in a cute restaurant and bar called Sweet Basil's. We booked for dinner and got a table right up near the band. It was such a cool place that you just couldn't help but have fun. The band was called Maggie and the Cats and they were playing everything from 'Brown Eyed Girl' to 'Proud Mary' and 'Moondance'. Scott had a couple of beers and got a little excited. One of his favourite songs came on and he said, 'Let's dance!' I was a little hesitant but he said he would get up without me, which would have been even more embarrassing. We hit the floor and we rock'n'rolled. My mother had taught me how to dance when I was little and I had passed my skills on to him. The people were in awe of us and we're not even that good. We felt like rock stars. To make the night even sweeter a guy said to my husband, 'Your wife is a beautiful woman.' Scott reluctantly passed on the compliment only because I asked what he said! I think the man might have had his beer goggles on but I was happy to run with it anyway. I'll never forget that night. Maggie from Maggie and the Cats and her partner, Richard, are now dear friends. Sweet Basil's is our favourite bar on earth.

I was having fun whenever I could in those days because I didn't know how many more days I had up my sleeve. What a memorable night. What an amazing weekend. What a special place.

Then it was time to go back to the city to learn my fate.

Chapter Twenty-seven

That Sunday night was punishing. My mind flicked from the scans, the results, the phone call from the doctor to fretting about my daughters being thousands of kilometres away when they hated being without us. If it wasn't bad enough that I wasn't there, I had now taken their father away from them. I felt so guilty. I didn't sleep a wink.

Night became day. The day I wanted to hear those magic words, 'You have responded.' I wanted everything to be gone from my body. I wanted to go home to my children.

What I didn't want to hear was that my tumours were growing, that the treatment wasn't working and I might as well go home to Australia and spend the rest of my days with family. I wanted to go home, but not like that.

We drove to the hospital and made our way to the Providence imaging department. I drank the radioactive liquid, then waited for an hour before I could have the scan. We amused ourselves by watching a man pulling faces and dry-retching every time he took a sip of his pre-scan concoction. I drank mine like it was apple juice. By then I was a seasoned pro.

I had the scan and we left. Doctor Urba had told us he would ring us in the next few hours with the results, and promised to mark our file 'Urgent'. He knew we were beside ourselves.

As a distraction we went to a travel agent and looked at some brochures of places we wanted to visit, but I felt sicker and sicker, more anxious and nauseous. This was it. Our ten months of hell had led us to this point. I did a quick thank you to my body and mind for getting me there. That was a feat in itself.

The information we were about to receive would determine if I lived or died. It was really that black and white. Even if I was responding there was no guarantees of longevity, but I had to put that thought out of my head. *One step at a time*, the sensible monster muttered, surprising me. He hadn't made an appearance for a while.

It was 3.30pm and we were back in our hotel room. I was sitting on our bed reading the same page of *Hello* magazine over and over again when the local phone rang. My heart leapt into my throat then every cell, muscle, organ and vein in my body started moving. We knew who it was. Scott answered and said, 'Hi Walt.' It was Doctor Urba. Scott had taken it upon himself to call him by his first name. 'I'll put her on,' he said.

I was shaking. 'Hi Doctor Urba,' I managed to get out. I was staring into Scott's eyes.

'You have responded,' he said, just like that. I started to howl. Oh my god, he had said it, those words that had circulated in my head for months along with the other version I was regularly reminded of – 'I'm sorry Julie, the drug isn't working for you.' But it was the good version. I felt numb, happy, sad, elated; I didn't know what the fuck I was feeling. I handed the phone back to Scott, who put the phone on loudspeaker. I was trying to keep my sobs quiet so he wouldn't hear. He was quite matter-of-fact. Just another day in the office for him, but for us it could have been Armageddon.

He went on to say, 'It's a good result but it's not great . . . yet. You have had a small reduction in most of your tumours, so we just need to keep going with the treatment.' He explained that some patients in the trial have everything disappear right away, but for others it can take longer *or* some respond for a little while then stop responding. I hit the metaphorical delete button on that last bit.

We made an appointment to see him at the hospital the following day to discuss the results in more detail and talk about our fundraising ventures. Then we thanked him three or four times before hanging up.

I was relieved, ecstatic, elated, happy, yes, in one way, but in typical Julie style I was disappointed that all my tumours hadn't disappeared. I didn't like having any tumours in my body, but who would? It sounds ridiculous but I had made peace with those tumour cells pretty much from the beginning as I really didn't want to upset them. We would just have to keep going with the treatment until my cells were ready to restore themselves to perfect health. But it also made me realise I wasn't going home to my family any time soon and that was hard to come to terms with. If all of my tumours had disappeared like they did for some patients, we probably would have packed our bags there and then.

We called home that afternoon and gave everyone the happy news. My girls were, well, relieved, is probably the only word for their emotions that day. I promised them I would 'fix it' and I had always kept my promises, so it was like they expected it. I loved that.

The thing was that they just wanted me home, us home, and back to normal. My sisters and brother were ecstatic. My baby sister, Nicole, just sobbed and sobbed when I told her. I thought she wasn't going to stop, although she later admitted to having a hangover from the night before and she was tired and emotional. We had a good chuckle about that.

Scott and I stared at each other for a while, then we wandered up the road for a little celebration at a quaint Japanese restaurant. Scott said he was never in any doubt, he knew the results would be good.

I replied, 'Really, who are you, Nostradamus?' We cuddled, crying and laughing at the same time. It was such a relief to relax for a while without thinking about cancer and living and dying at five-minute intervals. I had to give myself some time out. We talked about our next adventure. We decided we would go up to Seattle, which was across the border into Washington

State and 278 kilometres north of Portland. We would take off after our appointment with Doctor Urba the next day.

Those days were the best and worst of times rolled into one. My life was in the balance but we were exploring these exciting new places that we would never have seen under any other circumstances. We had to find the good in the very, very bad.

Doctor Urba was upbeat and happy as always. It was uplifting to see him so positive about my results. He casually repeated there were no guarantees that the drug would continue to work, but he did feel we were on the right path. We also made a plan to meet with the marketing team about making the videos. The nice monster congratulated me that day in the doctor's office. He said, *Told ya!* I smiled wearily because by then I felt a little jaded and tired, like I had permission to rest for a while, just a little while. I had earned it; *we* had earned it; and I realised a small section of the grey cloud that had infiltrated the inside of my skull had floated away.

Scott was a little taken aback when I blurted out, 'I want to go home, Doctor Urba. How can I get this drug back in Australia? I miss my girls, my family and friends.'

I thought he might answer with, 'Are you kidding me? You begged and pleaded and pestered us to take part in this two-year study for the very sake of saving your life. You have been here for five minutes and you want to go home. Are you serious? You signed up for a science project, girl. What are you thinking?'

But he didn't, he just calmly said, 'For now you need to stay. But I will do anything I can and stay in touch with the drug company to try to find a way to get you home to your people.

They do have very strict protocols as you can imagine, but we can only keep trying.'

He is a beautiful man, my second favourite in the world, as I've said. Well, equal second anyway, alongside my dad and my brother.

'Thank you,' I said through the usual flurry of tears.

We hit the I5 highway and made our way north to Seattle. I remember a feeling of real peace that afternoon and silently practised some gratitude. I had meditated in front of my vision board that morning and could see myself somewhere in my future. It seemed a little clearer than the last time.

It was rainy and cold when we drove into Seattle but I instantly loved the feel of the place. It reminded me of San Francisco with the long steep roads leading down to a pier at the bottom with restaurants, shops and bars. It was very cool indeed.

We went up to the top of the Space Needle, which is a massive observation tower similar to Sydney Tower. It has 360-degree views of the city, Mount Rainier and the rest of the surrounding ranges. We had a beautiful seafood dinner down at the pier and checked out Pike Place Fish Market, which is a famous tourist destination. When you purchase a fish they toss it from one side of the room to the other before they wrap it. Why? Because they were going broke and had to work out a way to sell more fish. It worked! There were people everywhere queuing to buy fish.

We returned to the bar at the Marriott Hotel (where we were staying) that night for a coffee and got chatting to the barman. A hip-looking guy with dreadlocks in a ponytail, he was asking us all about Australia and just like everyone else we spoke to in

America, Australia was on his bucket list. We picked his brains about things to do in the area and he convinced us that we would love the San Juan Islands. We had never heard of them before, but he painted a splendid picture.

We did some research when we went back to our hotel room. The San Juan Islands are an archipelago in the northwest corner between the US mainland and Vancouver Island in British Columbia, Canada. They looked amazing and there was so much to do. No-brainer, we were going.

Scott was a little cranky the next morning as the banging of the airconditioning had disturbed his sleep. He felt it necessary to mention this on checkout and it soon became obvious why. The receptionist apologised and as we were silver cardholders for Marriott Hotels she offered us compensation. But he couldn't leave it there. I knew what he was going to say. I was thinking, *Don't say it, don't say it!* Then, on cue, he proclaimed at the top of his voice, 'I was sleepless in Seattle!' The young girl laughed politely, like no one had ever said it before. I cringed and took a few steps away from him. Scott thought he was hilarious. He loves to crack up at his own jokes. At least someone thinks he's funny!

Later that morning we put the car on the ferry and off we went. It felt so freeing to be able to do something spontaneous like that. While I silently wished it was under different circumstances, I was determined to enjoy every moment of this little adventure. The day was raining and grey but the water still seemed magical and mesmerising. Our first hop was to Bainbridge Island, a sweet place with a quaint township.

There was a fundraising sausage sizzle in a carpark so we mixed it up with the locals and got some tips on the best places to visit. We pushed on and decided to stay in a place called Port Townsend. Not so pretty, but it got us closer to the next island hop. We booked a room, checked in and then went looking for somewhere to have dinner. We saw a sign in the corner of an obscure little carpark. It simply said 'Tavern', so we thought we'd have a look. Boy, did we get a shock. There were people everywhere. They were mostly our age, *and* there was live music. It was one of the coolest establishments we had ever seen and we had a fantastic night dancing and chatting to everyone. We both just love stumbling upon places like that and Oregon and Washington State seemed to be full of them.

Next stop was San Juan Island; now that place is picturesque. We booked a room in Friday Harbor, the main township where the ferry landed. We went fishing then hiked to the top of Young Hill and could see all the way over to Canada. The sun was shining that day. We were in a happy place.

Chapter Twenty-eight

On the way back to Portland, Scott nervously broached the subject of him going home to Australia in the next four or five days. He had to get back to work and the girls, the house and the dog. I had been on a semi-high for the past five days and that statement brought my world crashing down again. I knew it was coming but, like the cancer, I wished it would go away.

I went silent. My body responded with all those feelings of despair that had become so familiar. I stared out the car window, petrified of being alone again. I just wanted him to stay. He put his hand on my leg and I gently lifted it off. Then I said, 'I'm sorry', and started with the waterworks.

He needed to be home. I knew that. I wanted him to be home with our girls, too. I missed them like crazy. I hadn't seen

Morgan in two and a bit months and Remy since she'd left five weeks earlier. I missed my puppy dog.

Then suddenly I had an idea. *I will just go with him. I will have my treatment that week and I will go home and see my girls and come back for my next infusion two weeks later.* I was too scared to say anything to Scott as the elation of going home had washed over my whole body and I wanted the feeling to stay just where it was. He would bring up the money factor and rightly so, but money meant nothing to me at that time. I just wanted to hug my children, see my sisters and brother, cuddle my dad and take Roxy out to the park. I wanted to see my friends and the beach and be in my home and my bed.

I took a deep breath and said, 'I'm coming. I'm coming home with you to see the girls.'

'You won't be allowed,' he said

'Why?' I responded.

'Darl, we worked very hard to get you here, you don't want to fuck it up now. For god's sake you have had some success, that is all we have wanted from the start.'

'Yes,' I said, 'I am well aware of that, but what if that's it? What if I don't get any further response? What if I don't get to six months? And I am spending all this time away from my family?'

Scott didn't know how to answer those questions. Then he came out with one of his all-time favourite sayings, which annoys the crap out of me. 'I don't have a crystal ball, darl.' What does that actually mean? Even if he had one he wouldn't be able to predict the future. They're a bloody myth. I went quiet but I had not changed my mind.

The next day while Scott was in the shower I called Doctor Urba – he had given me his mobile number when he knew I was on my own. He answered my call on the second ring. I was so nervous but I had to ask the question. 'Doctor Urba, if I have my treatment this week and then go home to see my family, then be back in two weeks, would that cause a problem?'

'Well,' he said, 'the drug company don't like people flying as there have been cases of respiratory problems in patients and it is thought that high altitude heightens the risk.'

My heart sank. I was devastated and then he said, 'But in saying that . . . you are fit and healthy besides the obvious, so . . .'

'Okay,' I said, 'pretend this call never happened.' I'm pretty sure I told him I loved him that morning, and I meant it.

I hung up the phone and started screaming and dancing around the room. Scott came out of the bathroom asking what the hell was going on. I told him what I had done, but I accidentally left out the bit about the respiratory thing. Whoops! He seemed a little perplexed and concerned but he knew he couldn't fight me. I have never been so excited about a long-haul flight in my life. We booked our flights right away. I called Morgan and Remy and told them the news. They were both absolutely thrilled that we would all be back together again, even if it was only for eleven days as the flying hours would eat into my time at home. I called my dad and my sisters and brother and texted my friends. It was the happiest I'd been in a long time.

I would be home for Mother's Day!

I was counting down the hours and the minutes like a five-year-old before their birthday, but we were kept busy moving out of the hotel we had called home since we'd arrived in Portland. My dad had been so generous in wanting us to be comfortable, but we just couldn't sustain the expense any longer. As much as we didn't want to, we had to take up the offer of staying in the guest housing that was subsidised by the hospital – the old, cold, gloomy building I mentioned earlier. Thank god I was going home with Scott because if I had to stay in that place on my own I really don't know how I would have coped. The unit on offer was a little better than the one that had originally been available. At least it was above ground. It was on the first floor, across the road from the Cancer Center. I don't want to sound ungrateful because we weren't. We were thankful they could help us out, because we were going backwards financially at a hundred kilometres an hour. Scott found it comforting that I would be so close to the hospital when I was there on my own. For me the thought of being there alone was incomprehensible. I threw that notion into the too-hard basket. I had become adept at that.

The apartment, and I use the term very loosely, was up a rickety flight of stairs. When you opened the door, straight ahead you had a small, old kitchen with lino flooring, green floral wallpaper and a little round dining table. To the left was a dark brown velvet sofa and two reclining chairs on top of some orange and brown carpet. Down the hall there was a 1950s bathroom to the right, a bedroom to the left with dark brown everything and another bedroom with two wrought-iron single beds featuring the same lino as the kitchen. I didn't feel great being in there. When I look back now it probably wasn't that bad, but at the time anything that wasn't home just felt wrong, especially when I was on my own. What it did do, though, was ignite a passion to help raise money to build new apartments for the patients and their families who would come after me.

For now, this would be my new Portland home and I would just have to deal with it. Doctor Urba told me he had stayed there 20 years earlier and considered it old and drab then. We had been spoilt at the Marriott and it was time for a reality check. We moved our belongings, of which there were not many, then drove down to Fred Meyer, a huge department store, to pick up a few knick-knacks to make our new abode a little more homely.

When treatment day arrived, our bags were packed and ready to go by the door. We walked across to the hospital and checked in. I found it hard to disguise my excitement – I was jumping out of my skin but I think I pulled it off. Amy was my nurse that day and we chatted about her study and her boyfriend and her dream of coming Down Under. Then we heard the beeps of the machine that controlled the timing of my PD-1 infusions, which meant I was done. They flushed out my portacath with saline, put a dressing on my chest and said, 'See you in two weeks.'

'Are you folks travelling anywhere?' Amy asked. She was used to us telling her where we had been since my previous treatment.

'Yes,' I responded, 'we'll definitely go somewhere.' It felt good that we didn't tell a lie; after all, we were going somewhere.

We returned to the new dwelling, called a cab, grabbed our bags and we were off to Portland airport. It felt clandestine, like a covert operation you see in the movies. Euphoria swept over me. I would be home cuddling my precious baby girls in less than 24 hours.

Chapter Twenty-nine

Letter to Mum in Heaven

Hi Mum,

Guess what? I have responded to the treatment in America! My tumours are shrinking.

I think I just heard you say, 'Thank god, Jule,' and I know you are crying.

Me too, Mum. I am so happy I can tell you good news.

It's not a full response YET, but I just have to keep going. Guess what else, I am sneaking home to see the girls and the family. I am so bloody excited. Being away and trying so hard to save my life is by far the most difficult thing I have ever done and I can't believe how much I have put the family through in this last eleven months. But you know what, Mum, the funny thing is that after all this, I still feel lucky.

Lucky to have had you as a mum. Lucky to have Dad, my sisters and my brother, Scott and the girls, and bloody lucky that this treatment is working for me so far. At least I can breathe and regather and then push on to get the job done for good. The drug I am on is in its infancy so they don't have a lot of data to know what the future holds for patients, but it's all I have and apart from this really mean monster that gets in my head and says awful things to me, I am staying positive and hanging in there.

But what if it does stop working, Mum, what am I gonna do then? It will keep working, won't it, Mum? It has to!

I can't wait to be home, Mum. I have never felt so home-sick. It just adds to the pain and I miss everyone so much. My doctor is amazing and the nurses are all beautiful and caring. But it's not home.

Remy went back, about a month ago, she'd had enough. I don't blame her. Scott had to go with her. I was in total despair when they left. Thank god my friend Deb came over to stay with me. I am so blessed to have a great support team. I am a lucky girl, I really am.

Scott has been amazing, rock solid, Mum. Just like Dad. I'm so glad Scott's mine. Our marriage hasn't always been a picnic but I wouldn't swap him for anyone.

I guess the upside is that he feels too sorry for me to argue! So what I say goes, which is fun.

I remember when I asked you when I was younger what it was like to be married with kids. You said it was 'different'. Thanks for that, Mum, because if you had told me the real story I never would have contemplated it and it would be a real bummer not having Scott by my side right now.

You also used to say that you never felt grown up. No different from when you were 25. I feel the same way, just like a kid. My kids think I'm pretty lame most of the time and they cringe a lot, but that's okay. I think they kinda like it underneath. I've never understood those women who get to a certain age and then suddenly they're all sensible and grown up. That didn't happen to me. Maybe when I'm 51. Who knows, Mum.

I still feel like a child who needs her mother. I love writing to you. In fact, I love writing, period. I have actually promised the universe that when I get through this ordeal I will write a book. Yes, I know I'm not a writer, Mum, but surely I can tell a story. Even if just one person reads it then at least I have kept my promise.

There has to be some meaning to all of this or it just doesn't make any sense. If I could just help one person find a better treatment, or not take life for granted and drop the fear and do the things they are putting off for another day, then this whole debacle would at least have some meaning.

Anyway love and miss you more than words can say. I'll write again soon.

Love Jule xx

Chapter Thirty

We boarded the flight at around 10pm. Due to Scott's very frequent flyer points we were upgraded to premium economy, which was a nice surprise. I loved having more space, so our upgrade added to my excitement. The mean monster tried to remind me that I might have breathing difficulties and maybe even die mid-flight. I quickly responded by saying, *Not even you can rain on my parade tonight*, then promptly ordered a brandy. I was feeling like a naughty schoolkid playing hooky when the plane took off. It was hard to believe I was going back to Australia but would be back in Portland in two weeks sitting once again in my 'reserved for research' chair. I tried not to think about that.

Feeling rather relaxed after the brandy, I started a conversation with the man across the aisle. He was a doctor, and said he had his medical bag in the overhead locker. That was good news. I also figured that I could just use one of those masks that drop down from the ceiling if I felt short of breath. I am happy to report none of that was needed.

Scott and I both managed to get some sleep and woke up to a lovely bacon and egg breakfast. I was so hyped up, as Dad and my sister Nicole were picking us up at the airport. Remy had an early exam, which I pleaded with her to attend. Morgan had a dance class to teach, so I had also asked her not to come, saying we would all meet up at home. That's what I wanted. Scott and I secretly thought there might be a big crew at the airport with balloons and banners, maybe even a marching band. Well maybe not the marching band but we were expecting a few people. When we disembarked I ran to the bathroom to put on some make-up and comb my spiky hair. I wanted to look as healthy and well as I possibly could. We were both nervous and excited and trying to guess who would be there.

We grabbed our bags, got through Customs and made our way to the arrivals gate. Looking, looking, looking and nothing, there was no one there. No family, no friends, no balloons, no welcome home signs and no marching band. Not even my father and sister, who were still trying to find a parking spot. We had been gone ten weeks but it felt like ten years, and we felt like we were Olympians who had won gold and should be treated as such. I did always say that I just wanted people to treat me as per normal and not make a fuss, so that's what they did. Boy did we have a good laugh about that afterwards.

My family is renowned for being late and that morning was no exception. My sister and Dad had been arguing all the way to the airport, taking wrong turns and getting lost. We finally found them and all was forgiven. My dad hugged me so tightly I thought I was going to snap in half. I could tell Nicole was fighting back tears when she hugged me, but she held it together and we joked and laughed all the way home. It would be an hour or so before we saw Morgan and Remy, but I knew I would be greeted by my precious little Roxy. When we arrived home, the sun was beaming and there wasn't a cloud in the sky. It was almost winter but it was still warmer than Portland in autumn.

I left Scott to unload the bags and ran down our driveway. I was home. I opened the front door and there she was, my beloved golden retriever. She was priceless, yelping, barking and going crazy as she ran outside onto the driveway, then she did a little welcome dance and proceeded to go around and around in circles and run back to me, jumping up and down. She couldn't believe her mummy was home. Finally she flopped onto the floor, exhausted, puffing and panting with the biggest smile I had ever seen.

I was on my second cup of tea when I heard Morgan's car outside. I looked through the blinds and started jumping up and down. Running out to the car, I opened the door and literally pulled her out of the driver's seat. I was home, embracing my beautiful first-born child who had been so brave and stoic, holding the fort while we were gone. She simply said, 'Hi Mumma, I've missed you so much. I wish you didn't have to go back.'

'Me too,' I said. 'Let's enjoy every moment we have together.' Remy arrived home after her exam not long afterwards and I hugged the breath out of her as well. It felt like forever since I'd seen her, which was far too long. 'Hi Mummy,' she said, 'so glad you're home.'

Scott and I had never left the girls for more than a few days prior to all of this craziness. We'd figured we would have plenty of time for travel later when they were older. Luckily we didn't have one of those crystal balls Scott bangs on about because if we did and they did actually tell the future, then we would both be in the loony bin. Our travel plans had gone in a completely different direction.

The family came around that night, as was mandatory, and we showed a few travel snaps of Cannon Beach and the San Juan Islands. Everyone brought yummy dishes as they knew I wasn't much of a cook. I assured them there had been no dramatic improvements in the past ten weeks. My signature dish is 'chicken roll-up': I'll buy a chicken, you roll up and eat it. Simple, but effective.

I couldn't believe I was home looking at everyone again, laughing with everyone again. *Look at you*, said the nice monster. *Look what you've done. You had good results* and *you've got yourself home to your family.*

Yep, thanks, I replied, *but I'm not done yet.*

Mother's Day on Sunday 12 May 2013 was the best in my history of Mother's Days. Scott cooked breakfast and we sat out on the deck. The girls argued and Roxy ate the scraps off the ground. I was in heaven. I took Roxy out to chase the rabbits so

I could run and sing my song. Scott's mum came for lunch. She had been wonderful, having helped us out financially and with the girls. We were extremely grateful to her and by that stage I had forgiven her for her outburst in the kitchen that fateful morning eleven months prior.

That afternoon we went down to Narrabeen Lake with my whole family to celebrate Mother's Day for our own much-loved and missed mum. It was there that I had a crazy conversation with my sister Kerri. She said that the NSW State of Origin touch football coach had heard I was back in town and he would love me to play in the Over 45s Ladies tournament against Queensland the following weekend. I had missed out on it the year before, as it was two weeks after my diagnosis. The tournament was scheduled for the following Friday and Saturday. It was mind-blowing but exciting that I could actually be playing touch football again at that level. I knew I was a sympathy addition to the team, but so what? I had a spot and I had kept pretty fit in Portland.

The only problem was it would eat into my time with the girls. They heard the conversation and got really excited that I would be playing touch again, just like I used to. Like the mum they knew and loved. They wanted me to go more than I did myself.

But what if I got injured? That wouldn't be good. Then in my usual style I just thought, *Eff it, I'll do it.* The idea of running around a touch football field again feeling free and like a normal person was irresistible. Scott encouraged me to go for it.

That first week at home felt like a day, which was always the opposite feeling to my time in Portland when I was away from my family and friends. I squeezed in everyone and everything I could. The girls would run with me whenever they were around. I needed to be as fit as possible. I think my girls could see a glimpse of life as it used to be. I had promised them it would get back to normal and I was on a mission to keep that promise. It seemed that me playing in the tournament meant a lot of things to a lot of people.

We arrived at the oval in Coffs Harbour (on the New South Wales north coast) just in time for the team photo. It was surreal that I was standing there with them with NSW written on the front of my playing strip and number six on the back. All the girls hugged and kissed me telling me how proud of me they were. Nervous? You bet I was, but not the you're-going-to-die type of nervous. More, the you're-going-to-make-a-fool-of-your-self nervous, which was a tad easier to deal with.

The hooter went, it was game time. Queensland had the ball on the other side of the field and within ten seconds one of their players was sprinting down the sideline with one of our NSW players trying to catch her. I don't know what possessed me but I took off from the other side of the field as fast as my legs could carry me. I was gaining and gaining on this girl as she sprinted down the other side of the field. I'm sorry to say I didn't catch her; she put the ball over the try line just before I touched her. But I couldn't remember running that fast in years. Nobody could believe it. My sisters were laughing and crying simultaneously and all my teammates were asking me to get them some of the drug I was on.

Playing team sport is magical because for that hour you don't think of anything else but the game, and I welcomed that opportunity with open arms. I didn't do anything particularly brilliant for the rest of that series, but I was there, it was a part of my old life and it inspired me to keep going until I was back in that life for good.

We won the series for the fifth year in a row. I emailed a photo of me in my playing gear to Doctor Urba; he responded with, 'You are funny *and* stupendous.'

On the way home back to Sydney reality struck, and hard. In three days' time I would be packing to go back to America by myself. No Scott, no Morgan, no Remy, just me. I didn't want to go back alone but I had no choice. I had squeezed in an appointment with the professor at the Melanoma Institute to touch base and see if there had been some miracle that would allow me to stay home. She was so happy to see me alive and well and had a giggle that I had snuck home and played touch footy.

There was no miracle. The professor was lovely and encouraging, telling me how well I looked and to keep going. It sounded so simple just to 'keep going', but the truth was nobody knew if I would keep going and keep responding to the drug. These trials were still in stage one so they had little evidence of what might happen down the track.

I was leaving my nearest and dearest once again when I wanted to be with them more than any other time in my life.

But it was short-term excruciating pain for long-term gain. That's what I told myself over and over again.

My friend Liz was in Amsterdam on a business trip with her husband at that time and was due to arrive home the day before I left. When I saw her name come up on a Viber message I thought she would be trying to arrange a catch-up before I left. But what I saw was a message that totally lifted my spirits, as I had been sliding further and further into despair as my departure time approached.

'Hello Julie, I will be back on Wednesday morning and I'll fly back to Portland with you the next day and stay with you for a week.' I could not believe it. Now that *was* above and beyond the call of duty, but I accepted her kind gesture with open arms. I gave her the flight details and she managed to get herself a seat. I will never forget what an expression of true friendship that was. People were using their hard-earned annual leave to be with me on the other side of the world so I wasn't alone.

Departure day arrived and I said goodbye to my girls again, pepping them up and telling them that soon this would all be a distant memory. I asked them to help their father and look after each other while dealing with a lump in my throat that felt bigger than Texas.

Scott picked up Liz then drove us to the airport. I have tears in my eyes as I am writing this because every time I said goodbye to him my heart felt like it was being ripped out of my chest. Liz was trying to comfort me by saying we could have a free breakfast in the Qantas lounge, god love her.

There was no easy way to do it, so I asked him to just drop us off and keep going. I didn't want him to come inside the terminal, it would be too hard. We pulled up at Departures and he got our bags. We looked at each other. I could see the sadness in his deep blue eyes. I cuddled him tightly. I never wanted to let go but I did. I didn't turn around as Liz and I walked through the automatic doors to the check-in area. I had no idea when I would hold him again.

The flight was long but uneventful and I had warned Liz about the accommodation at the other end. Thank god I had her with me, as I would have been in a state of despair going back to that place on my own. They called it 'the apartment' at the hospital so I followed suit, in jest. It was no such thing in my eyes, nor would it be in any other Australian's eyes as we use that title for a more upmarket style of dwelling. It was affordable housing and I was grateful for that. It's just that I am one of those people whose mood changes with my surroundings, but I was working hard to keep everything in perspective. Our knick-knacks from Fred Meyer did brighten up the place a little.

It was about 3pm when we arrived there. We dumped our bags, fell onto a single bed each and crashed out. We had set our alarms for 6pm because we wanted to go for a walk while it was still light and find somewhere to have dinner. It was almost summer, so the sun was making a regular appearance, which made things a little more bearable. I had only spent one night at the apartment before we flew home so I wasn't overly familiar with the surroundings. It turned out that when we turned right instead of left as we had done to go to the Cancer

Center, we came across a gorgeous, picturesque neighbourhood with oak trees aplenty and squirrels everywhere running up the trunks and returning with nuts in their mouths. The houses were stunning, olde worlde and colourful with porch swings and garden gnomes. I can honestly say that neighbourhood is one of the prettiest I have ever seen and was to become part of my healing and wellbeing, and a godsend when I was living there alone.

Liz and I walked along admiring the vista and the vibe. Since the weather was warmer there were kids outside under sprinklers and mums and dads chatting with their neighbours. It was a side of Portland I hadn't seen and it was growing on me by the minute. We got lost trying to find a restaurant I had driven past a few times called Pambiche. It was in a bright-blue, fun-looking building with Cuban cuisine. We called Scott in Australia and he talked us through directions from Google maps. Gotta love technology. We had to wait about twenty minutes for a table, but boy was it worth it. The food was amazing. We shared lamb shanks and black beans and a hearty Cuban stew. I love that food. When we left the restaurant we heard music coming from across the road so we toddled over to have a look. It was a bar/restaurant called Blue Agave, which was heaving with people dancing to salsa music, laughing and generally having a fabulous time. Liz and I joined in and had a fun night. I was so happy she was enjoying herself after the massive sacrifice she had made to be with me. I made a friend, Katie, who worked at Blue Agave and it became one of my go-to places.

When we arrived home that night I noticed in the mirror that my eyes had become a little grey and I had more bags than usual. I just wrote it off as jet lag and hopped into bed. Being rather exhausted, we both managed to get some sleep in our little wrought-iron cots. The next morning we got up, grabbed a cuppa and crossed the busy highway, making our way to the Cancer Center. I was ready to get some more of the PD-1 into my system; after all, that's what the whole thing was about, right? We went upstairs in the lift to the sixth floor as usual, walked into reception and Patti greeted us with the usual 'G'day', the greeting Scott and I had taught her.

I introduced Liz as my friend who had just flown in from Australia. I wasn't lying. I just left out the bit about me being on the plane with her. I checked in, stating my birthday backwards as they liked you to do over there, then waited for my name to be called. But this time I wasn't called to get my routine weigh-in, blood pressure test, etc. I was called into the clinic. I said 'Hi' to all the nurses, introduced Liz and sat in my usual chair. Nurse Amy came over with a slightly troubled look on her face and said, 'Hey Julie, I just have to call Daniel, he wants to talk to you.'

'Oh, what for?' I asked.

'Your thyroid is out of whack.'

'What does that mean?'

'Not sure, you'll have to ask Daniel.'

I sat there rather perplexed. I knew about the thyroid, but I wasn't really sure what it did. After about five minutes, Daniel walked into the clinic. He came over, sat down and said,

'Unfortunately we can't give you your infusion today because your thyroid is out of balance.'

'What?'

'The drug company sent an email that said, "re: Patient 71, basically no more drug until the thyroid is under control".' Daniel looked upset giving me the news.

'When did you know about it?' I enquired.

'They have just told us now that it showed in your last blood test.'

'So when can I get it?' I asked, a little concerned.

'They want to test your levels again in two weeks.'

'Two weeks?' I almost shouted.

To say I was devastated would be skimming the surface. I had left my husband and children and dragged my friend across the Pacific to stay on protocol and on schedule to get my drug, the one I hoped was working away inside me, melting all my tumours, and I was told I couldn't have it. I actually didn't need to be there; I could have been home with my girls and my husband for another two weeks.

I couldn't hide my despair. I tried to hold it together for Liz's sake, but I couldn't. I lost it. She put her arm around me and we left. Thank god she was with me, otherwise I really don't know what I would have done. It was beyond upsetting as neither of us needed to be there. Liz could have flown back with me two weeks later. We went back across the road, and I sat on my wrought-iron bed and called Scott, bawling my eyes out. 'Why didn't someone tell me?' I kept saying over and over again. But they didn't know I was at home. They didn't realise what a huge impact it would have on my world. He said he would call and ask Doctor Urba and ring me back.

Poor Liz was out in the lounge room. 'Do you want a cup of tea? Are you hungry? Do you want to go for a walk?' she asked me. I just kept saying no, as I was gasping for breath between sobs. Then to top it off I realised it would be a month between treatments and that's *if* they could get my thyroid levels under control.

Liz then walked up to the shops to grab some supplies. I don't blame her for wanting to get out of there. The phone rang, it was Doctor Urba. 'Scott told me you're down in the dumps,' he said in his lovely American drawl.

Choking back the tears, I said, 'Yes, they wouldn't give me my treatment because of my thyroid.'

'Well,' he said, 'I've never seen that happen before and I am so sorry. But I can tell you that these issues mean that the drug has revved up your immune system and unfortunately it sometimes attacks your thyroid, but this usually means the drug is working. So I think it's a positive sign. Waiting another two weeks shouldn't affect anything.'

'Thanks so much, Doctor Urba,' I said. 'I'll see you soon.' Those were the only words that could have consoled me and I immediately pulled myself together. Liz was surprised but relieved when she returned that there had been a big shift in my mood. I told her what Doctor Urba had said.

'Thank god for that,' she said. She must have been envisaging the week from hell and counting down the days until she could escape.

Julie Randall

I enjoyed that week with Liz. Having just been in Europe, she wasn't really keen on the touristy thing so we just did some local Portland stuff. Shopping, restaurants, the Saturday markets in the city and one more go at the salsa dancing. Then it was time for her to go. I know she hated leaving me there alone but she had a husband, work and a family she had to get back to.

We walked up to Fred Meyer that morning to get my supplies for the week. Liz carefully chose the ingredients of simple meals she felt I was capable of producing and we walked home chatting and laughing all the way. On the inside, though, I was already hollow and lonely. This would be the first time I would be in my new home by myself and I hated that thought. I know there are millions of people who live alone, but I was thousands of kilometres away from my family and friends. I had been told more than once that anything could happen at any time with the disease I had inside me, so being on my own scared me senseless. I had to hang on to Doctor Urba's words that the drug was still working.

Chapter Thirty-one

Liz called a cab to the airport and it seemed like it arrived before she put the phone down. I helped her down the rickety stairs, twelve of them. I hugged her and thanked her with all my heart. Then I couldn't hold back the tears. She didn't want to get into the cab with me in that state, but she had a plane to catch. I promised her I would be okay then she climbed into the cab, waved goodbye and she was gone. I turned around and looked at this strange old building that was now my home and walked towards it, incredulous. Climbing up the stairs, I walked inside and sat on what was now my recliner chair, staring out the window at the office block across the street, sniffling, blowing my nose and feeling sorry for myself. It was a beautiful sunny day with a slight breeze – I was trying to look for some positives. *You knew this wasn't going to be a walk in the park so just toughen up, woman*, I told myself. I kept waiting for someone to knock at the door, but they didn't. No one was coming.

The nice monster started singing my song to me and encouraged me to push through. *You can do this*, he said, *you have done it before and you can do it again. Get outside and get some endorphins going, girl.* So that's what I did. I put on my exercise gear, locked the door behind me, climbed down the squeaky, rickety stairs and stepped out into the sunshine. I turned right instead of left to the hospital and ran down into my new little neighbourhood, singing the song that had helped me to get that far, with the lyrics I so desperately wanted to come true.

I am happy and healthy,
All my organs have healed,
My body and its organs have healed,
I have faith in life.

I came to love running and walking around that neighbourhood, especially passing the little primary school where I would watch the kids laughing and teasing each other and running around the playground. I loved listening to the teacher barking out orders and scolding them for being naughty. My thoughts would wander back to when my girls were little and I would get lost in those memories. All along the wire fence they had polystyrene butterflies that had been painted by the children in all shades of purple, pink and green. Thank goodness Liz and I turned right that day instead of left, as there is a good chance I may never have known it was there.

On my way back home I decided to pop into a shop to buy some soda water, when I noticed a building on the corner with a sign saying 'Portland Yoga Arts'. It was closed at the time so I grabbed a brochure and checked out the timetable. Wow, a yoga studio so close to home. Now that was a good thing. I had been doing yoga for the previous eleven months and still wasn't very good at it, but I loved it, concentrating on my breathing and executing the poses was a diversion that helped me keep my sanity.

Scott called me in the afternoon, which was his morning, to see how I was doing. Liz had called him from the airport, worried about my state of mind. I had calmed down and accepted that this was my home for now, I would be there by myself, and I would have to deal with it. My new focus was to stop moping around and start working out ways to stay positive and pass the time until I could be home again. I told Scott I was okay, but it was hard to talk to him without tearing up. I missed him so much I could feel it physically in my solar plexus.

Occupying the days was a struggle, not to mention the nights. Being a busy, working wife and mother for twenty-odd years prior to my world falling apart, it had always been the complete opposite. There was never enough time in the day to get everything done. I was as busy as a one-legged tap dancer!

That first day by myself was hard. I could write in my journal, that would take up about fifteen minutes. Yoga, one hour? Meditation, ten minutes? Yep, all up about an hour and a half. The groceries were already done for the week. Liz had been adamant we should get that done. I could go running again? Maybe walking? But I was already thin enough, I had to be careful not to lose any more weight. My 'Bill Diet' was a winner if you want to shed the kilos but I had already dropped five and I wasn't overweight to begin with. My arms and legs were skinny and with my spiky hairdo, I already looked like a plucked chicken.

I was pushing myself to harden up, but I almost always had an anxious, sick feeling in my stomach and a loneliness in my heart that I never knew existed, even though I had only been alone for a few hours. I was one of five children; I'd always had people around growing up. There were eight of us. Mum, Dad, Nanna Sharkey and the kids. Lonely? Never. It was hard to get a moment's peace. I used to spend a bit of time in the laundry, sitting on top of the washing machine, daydreaming, talking to imaginary characters and thinking about boys *and* getting some peace knowing that my brother and sisters would never come in. I don't think they knew the laundry was there.

On top of everything else, being alone in my new home was quite scary. I didn't have the security of a big hotel with 24-hour reception, nor did I have a fireplace to stare into and pass the time. I thought I had done it tough at the Marriott on my own but I soon realised that was almost a walk in the park. There were four other 'apartments' in the building with very sick patients and their carers. I had seen them coming and going, and at night I could hear the sirens of ambulances constantly transporting people to the Emergency Room.

I'd known I wouldn't feel safe with just a chain across the door as security, so Scott had put in brackets on either side of the doorframe the night before we left and demonstrated how, if I put a broom in each bracket, it would provide extra security from any rogue Portlandians who may try to break in and hurt me or steal my two-thirds of nothing. I had also planned to slide the table over in front of the door to create a fortress. To be frightened on top of everything else just wasn't an option.

I managed to get through the night in the old grey recliner that would became my bed. I couldn't sleep in either of the bedrooms, it just exacerbated my anxiety – I had to be next to the door so I could hear any noises. I tuned in to Jimmy Fallon and even found a little comfort in Joyce Meyer preaching the word of God to pass the time. I couldn't listen to music without Scott; it just made me sad. He told me he couldn't either during that time. I would leave the television on all night for company so when I woke up it felt like I wasn't alone.

I loved my own company back in the days before the sky fell in. I was never a person who has to have people around all the time but those days in Oregon were different. It was hard. I was constantly wrestling with the mean monster and negative thoughts, fighting back with my version of the story, which would end so differently from his. There weren't many distractions when I was there on my own. Sometimes it felt like it was just me and him.

Along with my husband, the nice monster congratulated me for being a brave girl and getting through the days in my new accommodation without incident. That evening when I was talking on the phone to my girls, they seemed a little more upbeat than usual and eager to put me back on to Scott. Then he blew me away by saying he and my brother had organised to fly my younger sisters, Michelle and Nicole, over to be with me on my birthday in a week's time. I knew my birthday was approaching but I hadn't given it much thought. When it did cross my mind it only brought back bad memories of what had happened the year before.

I was overwhelmed with excitement. I'd forgotten that emotion. It was such a huge lift. Scott was doing everything he possibly could to make my crazy world a little brighter. That surprise was just amazing. I could not believe my sisters were coming to stay with me in Portland in my luxury apartment.

It would be a week before they arrived for my birthday. That seemed like years away but it was something to focus on to get me through another passage of time. The thought that I would soon have close contact with my loved ones would almost take my breath away. During that week I didn't even try to live in the moment; I was transported to the future because having my sisters with me was far more appealing than the present.

At that stage I had been back in Portland for two weeks without any PD-1, my potentially life-saving drug. It was time for my next infusion, fingers crossed. I walked across the highway with trepidation as I was scared I might lose the plot if they said I still couldn't get it. They took my blood, and they had pathology on site so within ten minutes my results were back. My thyroid levels were good, the thyroid medication they'd given me had done the trick. The nurses hooked me up and I was away. What a bloody relief that was. Somewhere deep inside I was terrified they would kick me off the trial if I couldn't get my thyroid right. I had to keep getting this drug. I was hell-bent on keeping my promise to my daughters.

That week felt like slow motion personified, but I was doing an hour and a half of yoga every day, which was an absolute godsend. I can't tell you how excited I was feeling about seeing my sisters Michelle and Nicole who were due to arrive at 3.45pm on Friday 7 June 2013. I jumped on the light rail and made my way to the airport then waited anxiously for them to appear at the arrivals gate. Internally I was almost jumping up and down on the spot like a three-year-old. It felt like the whole planeload of passengers had disembarked except for them but just as I was becoming concerned, I saw them walking through the doors. I love my sisters so much and could not believe they were going to be with me for a whole seven days. *Now it's time to live in the moment*, I thought as they walked towards me, grinning.

After hugs and tears we sat down in a café and they gave me all the news from home. I felt some peace. We went back to my abode, where they presented me with birthday presents and cards. Scott had written some heartfelt words and bought me a beautiful purple pendant, and for the first time it hit me hard that I wasn't going to see him on my birthday. But I had my sisters. I wouldn't be alone.

The next day, 8 June 2013, was my 51st birthday. I took the girls into the city and to the Portland Markets. We giggled and smiled our way through the day. That night we decided to hit the city to celebrate. I had made it to 51 so I had a word with the mean monster, who had told me that may not happen.

See, I said silently, *I'm here*, and I poked my tongue out at him in the mirror.

I felt great that day. My hair was very short but cute, pixie like; the weather was amazing; I had my sisters with me. Life was okay. We caught the train to the city that balmy evening and popped into an Irish pub that was buzzing with atmosphere, then made our way across the street to a pub called the Red Lion, which Scott and I had heard good things about. Renowned for its great live music, it didn't disappoint. On the way over we noticed a large crowd lined up on either side of the road, cheering and clapping. Michelle gently pushed her way through the crowd then turned around and motioned for us to come over with a big cheeky grin on her face. Well, I have never seen anything so funny in my life. It turned out this was the annual Portland World Naked Bike Ride to protest against oil dependency and the overuse of fossil fuels. Talk about a laugh. I didn't know that people and their bits and pieces came in so many different shapes and sizes! Just when we thought we couldn't laugh any more, another bunch of nudies would cycle past showcasing another little *or* big surprise and we'd be off again, tears of laughter streaming down our faces. I'll never forget that night; it was one of my favourite birthdays for so many reasons. You hear the old adage 'Laughter is the best medicine' bandied about a fair bit, but it truly is. We all should think hard about how much we laugh and then find a way to laugh some more. Fun is underrated and having more of it is one of the big lessons I have taken out of this topsy-turvy roller-coaster ride.

I remember thanking the universe for my sisters that day and also for keeping me so strong and for allowing my body to handle the treatment so well. I could have been really sick like some of the other poor patients I had been told about and that really would have been the pits. I am not sure what part, if any, the universe had to play, but something felt like it was on my side that day.

Inevitably, the week went too fast and my beautiful sisters, like all my visitors, had to go home to their families and their jobs. Saying I was gutted does not describe the churning feeling overtaking my intestines. We wheeled their bags all the way down the street to the train station; I wanted to be with them as long as I possibly could so we all caught the light rail to the airport. They were going back home to the place across the Pacific Ocean where I desperately wanted to go. They would be seeing my daughters and I wouldn't be. It wasn't fair. I wanted to be getting on that plane so much that it brought me to tears. We sat at the bar trying to chat but I just felt flat, like I had been run over by a tractor. My poor sisters would have been just as distraught leaving me behind but kept trying to cheer me up with words of encouragement.

When their flight to LA was called, we stood up and walked slowly over to the security barriers. I hugged them both at least three times and demanded they hug my girls for me. Then I watched them as they went through the scanner, collected their bags and walked out of sight, waving as they went around the corner. I was alone again.

I was feeling well physically, but emotionally I was distressed. In a couple of weeks I would have more scans to monitor my progress. Remember the first time it was a 'good result but it's not great'? Well this time I wanted 'great'. Getting through the next six months would be crucial for my survival.

Feeling well in this game, unfortunately, was not necessarily what it seemed. After all, I had been on top of my game, on top of the world, when I fell down with a huge thud twelve months earlier. My mindset was as important as ever: I had to dig deep and stay strong. Walking away from my sisters, I made my way back to my apartment on the train feeling as hollow as a log.

Drawing on every bit of strength I had, I made it through the following week. When time zones allowed I talked to Scott and the girls as much as possible. I walked, ran, sang my song, did yoga, wrote in my journal and thumbed through fashion magazines, fantasising that I would be home and well soon, and somehow able to afford some stylish outfits.

Doctor Urba called and invited me to sit in on a lunch meeting with the fundraising team and most of the big sponsors who supported the hospital. As I've mentioned, Scott and I had agreed to help raise money for research and for the new guest housing project. It was wonderful to have this opportunity, but sitting through some of the data being presented was extremely confronting. The doctor was talking about the new and exciting world of immunotherapy, some of the great results they were seeing and how a third of patients were responding and have been given 'more time with their family and loved ones'. He then went back to a bar chart projected onto a screen. The bar chart showed advanced melanoma patients before the introduction of this new treatment through clinical trials. The mortality rate was 100 per cent. Not 95 or 98, but 100 per cent of patients died. Although I knew this was the case, seeing it there in black and white scared me. The lump in my throat grew larger and larger and the mean monster whispered, *I told you*. It felt like everyone in the room was staring at me, then the lady next to me said, 'You are so brave' and put her hand on my leg.

'I'm not brave,' I felt like saying. I didn't ask to get stage four cancer so I could challenge myself to cure it. That would be brave. I had no say in it – it was forced on me. I had no choice but to put one foot in front of the other and hope I was going in the right direction. Keeping it together that day was incredibly hard, but I had to. Doctor Urba wanted me to talk about the guest housing and what it would mean to future patients to have a new, modern, secure facility to stay in at such a vulnerable time of their lives. Somehow I managed to get through it but all I could think of were my next scans and how much trouble I would be in if they weren't good. I went home and gave my cells yet another huge pep talk.

My local phone rang soon after I arrived home that afternoon. It was Shari Scales, my angel from Providence. She told me that one of the volunteers from the hospital would like to take me out for lunch the following weekend; she had heard I was alone and thought I might enjoy some company. I gratefully accepted. Shari told me her name was Monique. 'She knows where you live and she will pick you up at 1pm on Sunday.'

'Okay great,' I replied. 'Thank you Shari for looking out for me.' I now had something to look forward to – I would have more human contact in a few days. I didn't know this person from a bar of soap and normally I would have wondered whether we would get along and if we would have anything in common, but at that point my friendship base was rather limited and I would have enjoyed the company of a Russian spy who didn't speak any English and grunted his or her way through the afternoon.

Sunday rolled around (very slowly) and in the morning I eagerly got myself ready for my lunch outing. Standing in the shower, I made up stories in my mind of who this woman would be and why she had so kindly offered to take me out for a meal. I figured she would be around 65 and a little stout. She would be driving an old car, probably a Morris Minor and would be wearing a frock, you know the style of frock with the pockets at the front so you can load them up with pegs when you're hanging out the washing. Her hair would probably be grey. She was a devoted volunteer, so she had no interest in styling, grooming and preening. I didn't overdo my outfit – a bright-orange T-shirt and white jeans. I always had to wear something bright in those dark times. For me it represented living.

Well, I could not have been any further off the mark with my made-up profile of Monique. At about 1.05pm I got a call. 'Hey Julie, it's Monique, I'm out the front.' I ran down the rickety stairs and out into the street. Parked in the driveway was a white Mercedes Benz sports car with tinted windows. Trying to disguise my shock, I walked quickly over and ran around to the passenger door. Well in Australia it was the passenger door, but in America it was the driver's door and I almost jumped in and sat on the poor woman's lap.

'Oh my god,' I said apologetically, 'I'm sorry, I'm used to jumping in this side.' I gently shut the door and ran to the other side. *This woman will think I'm a complete nutter!* I thought as I opened the door and climbed in. And there she was, one of the most beautiful women I had seen in real life. She had jet-black, long, wavy hair, dark golden skin and sea-green eyes. She was wearing a beautiful green floral top, making her eyes pop. I remember thinking she was a dead ringer for Wonder Woman!

'Where do you want to go? Do you like mojitos?'

Thank you God, this woman is speaking my language. 'Sure, I would love one!' Off we went. I had never been to the western part of Portland so it was fun to explore a new part of town, and it was so hip and cool, with a great atmosphere. We found a cosy restaurant and didn't stop talking for the next few hours. That afternoon was lovely; I felt slightly normal, like I was out with a girlfriend. I told her my story and she told me hers. Monique is a close friend now and I will forever be grateful to her and her husband, Ralph, who have been more than amazing to me and Scott.

Mo, as I learned was her nickname, dropped me back home that afternoon and asked me if I would like to have dinner and stay at her place sometime during the week. She laughed when I said I'd have to check my diary but I was sure I could fit it in. We arranged that she would pick me up after work the next

Thursday at around six. I met a friend that day just when I needed one the most.

To make my Sunday even better, Scott called and told me he had organised everything at home so he could fly over and be with me for my next scan in two weeks. As soon as he said those words my body reacted: I could feel my insides changing to happy. When he wasn't with me, there was an ache in my heart that nothing could fix.

As he said those words I also started worrying about the girls being without both parents again and so far away under hideous circumstances. The thought of being alone for my scan results, though, was also unbearable. Between a rock and a hard place? I was well and truly wedged. What if the results weren't good? What if the treatment had stopped working? How would I cope? I concluded I would have to just book the first flight home and make the long, lonely trip back to my family. But Scott said he was coming and no matter what I said, he wouldn't take no for an answer, and that's how I made it through the next couple of weeks.

Monique had asked for my email address and sent me through a menu from a place called Best Little Roadhouse. She and Ralph own the restaurant, which is in Salem, the capital of Oregon. This was a surprise to me – I thought it was Portland. Anyway it felt a little strange but I checked out the menu and placed my order for dinner for the following Thursday night. Ralph would bring home the meals from the restaurant.

Mo tooted the horn at 6pm on Thursday and we headed off down the highway towards her home. She lived north of

Portland in Washington State, in a town called Battle Ground. It is a stunning rural location, and was a welcome break from the city for me. She had a dark-brown horse called Peppy and a black and white cattle dog called Bear. It was a home, a real home where real people lived. It wasn't my home where my family lived but it was a home, nonetheless.

Ralph arrived with our dinner from the Roadhouse. I had ordered the buffalo wings that were yummy with a tasty ranch dressing, which is very popular in the States and probably a no-no on my diet, but I gave myself an exemption. Ralph is a great guy and it was so interesting to hear all his views on American politics. While I enjoyed being there with these kind and caring couple, having my own bedroom with gorgeous interiors, an ensuite and a flatscreen TV, nothing could take away my heartache, the isolation from my family and the unpredictability of my future. I was trying to keep positive, but the loneliness and despair were never far away.

Chapter Thirty-two

Mo dropped me back to Portland the next morning on her way to work and we arranged to catch up when Scott arrived in a couple of weeks. It would be another long and lonely fourteen and a half days.

Writing to Mum, doing yoga, staring at my vision board, getting lost in fashion magazines and running through my neighbourhood helped me cope. But one summer morning I thought my running days might have come to an abrupt standstill.

I had dropped a glass on the floor a couple of days before and had not swept it all up properly. Along with my lack of cooking skills, I'm not the best cleaner in the world either. Scott often used to say to me, 'If you put your glasses on, darl, you might actually be able to see what you're doing.' I usually told him to shut up, but now I was wishing I had taken his advice.

I stepped my right foot into the kitchen from the hallway and both my big toe *and* my heel caught two separate shards of glass. I don't do things in halves.

Oh shit! were the first words that came to mind. I couldn't put my foot on the ground and it hurt like crazy. I hopped to the couch and gingerly sat down, freaking out. Obviously I had been through a fair bit and had been forced to toughen up on many occasions, but I did not take kindly to having glass protruding from under my foot. I wanted to ring Scott and cry but it was the middle of the night for him, so the only thing I could do was try to make my way across the road to the hospital. I attempted to get dressed but I was shaking uncontrollably. Eventually I managed to pull on some shorts and a T-shirt and put a thong on my left foot. Grabbing my keys, I stuck them in my pocket, shut the door behind me, then stared at the staircase between me and flat ground. I lowered myself onto the floor and sat at the top of the stairs, then plonked down each stair like my girls did when they were little.

This was the first time I could remember having no one to help me in a crisis. At home there was always help available, at worst a few minutes away. As I bounced my way down the rickety stairs I hoped someone would come through the bottom door and rescue me, but they didn't. I couldn't call an ambulance or go to the ER because I wasn't insured in the US, so I had to make my way to the Cancer Center and ask one of the nurses to help me.

As I landed on the last step I figured out my next move, but by the time I made it to the door there was blood dripping heavily onto the floor. I opened the door and with a combination of hopping and turning my injured foot on the side to rest it I made it to the crossing. I thought a motorist might stop and help me, but that didn't happen. I made it to the other side of the busy highway and somehow limped into the foyer of the Cancer Center, where I slumped, crying, on a bench.

A volunteer reception man put me in a wheelchair and asked me where I needed to go. 'The sixth floor,' I managed to get out. He took me up and presented me to the nurses, who were quite startled to see me in that state. They removed the glass and bandaged the wounds. It wasn't their department, they didn't have to help me, but they knew my position. Nothing was said. They just cared for me like they always did with a smile and a hug.

Providence Cancer Center had become a spiritually important place for me. It taught me the meaning of benevolence and the true meaning of God. To me, 'God' is the part of us made up of true love and empathy. Everyone I met through Providence will go above and beyond the call of duty to make the world a little bit easier to bear and they trust they will receive love in return. I decided that day I would try hard to be more like them.

The fact that I had found *that* place and *those* people was a miracle in itself. Nurse Amy helped me home that afternoon, and I stayed inside for two days – my foot was too sore to walk or run or even navigate the stairs.

I had mentioned to Doctor Urba that Scott was coming back, and he asked if we would still be able to shoot the video to help raise money for cancer research at Providence. I said yes without hesitation; I wanted to do everything I could for him and his team. After all, they were giving me a chance at life *and* I knew Scott would be happy to get his melon on screen. I'm sure he's a wannabe actor and fancies himself as a Brad Pitt lookalike, as you know.

My stomach would fill up with butterflies every time I thought of seeing him walk towards me at the airport. I closed my eyes and imagined his big muscular arms wrapping around me and my head tucking into his chest. I would smell his smell and it would feel like home. The tears welled up in my eyes just thinking about it.

It was a warm Saturday afternoon in Portland with beautiful blue skies and I decided I was going to be brave and go out for dinner by myself. I would walk through my neighbourhood and down the highway and see my friend Katie at Blue Agave, the salsa bar and restaurant. I started out at 6pm and it was a 45-minute walk. I felt some happiness that evening; the arrival of my man was coming closer and I was proud of myself for getting out of the apartment – I was usually bunkered in around that time.

Katie give me a big smile when I walked in. I sat up at the bar and before I knew it I had a drink in front of me, closely followed by some tapas plates of ricotta mushrooms and Mexican chicken. She would tend to the needs of all the patrons but would always come over and talk to me in between. She was an attractive woman, with blonde hair and blue eyes. Although I never asked her, I guessed she was around 25. She was a single mother and did shifts at the bar to make ends meet. Her mother helped out with her little girl while she worked.

I watched sport on the big TV screen to fill in time between our chats and wondered what stories the other patrons were making up in their heads about why a middle-aged woman was in the bar alone. I figured they would have as much chance as winning the lottery thrice than guessing what the real story was. I amused myself with that little assumption. All of a sudden I realised it was growing dark outside and I had a 45-minute walk back to the apartment, so I quickly paid the bill, said goodbye to Katie and headed out to the street. I had been told not to walk alone at night so I started walking quickly, almost marching, cranky with myself for losing track of time. About fifteen minutes into the journey I could hear voices behind me, male voices. I could tell they were either drunk or high. Either way I had to get away from them. I picked up the pace and they must have noticed.

'Hey lady!' one of them called out. 'Where are you goin'? Wanna come with us?' I just kept marching. I was too far away to go back to the restaurant. 'Wait for us, lady! Do you wanna drink with us?' another asked in a Hispanic accent. I was terrified.

Please, please don't let me get raped and murdered after all of this, please, please, I was begging in my head. I had Mo's number on my local phone but she was an hour away. Anyway, I couldn't stop or even slow down. They kept calling out to me and I kept ignoring them. Should I flag a motorist? That could be worse. I could see a street coming up on the left which was a shortcut home. Not being able to decide whether I should take it or stay on the main road, my heart was pounding a hundred kilometres an hour. *You bloody idiot!* I was saying to myself over and over again.

In a split-second I made the decision. I was going to turn left and run as fast as I could. As far away as possible from those scary boys and all the way back to my home. I took the corner at normal pace and then I bolted, running as fast as I could through the dark streets. If they followed me I would jump over a fence and bang on a door and scream my lungs out. I could hear them back at the end of the street, laughing and jibing me, but I could tell they hadn't followed me so I just kept going. By now I was exhausted, puffing and panting, but very thankful that my frequent runs meant I was fit enough to go fast. I then slowed down to a walk, looking behind me the entire time. I had never been so happy to see my brown brick and timber home. In that moment it was Buckingham Palace. I ran up the rickety stairs, shoved my key into the lock, jumped in, locked the door, put up my broom, pushed over my table and piled the chairs on top. Then I sat on my recliner and tried to get my breath back. I wanted to cry but I couldn't, I was still in fight or flight mode. I couldn't believe what had just happened. Talk about living on the edge! I was making a career out of it.

Finally the day of Scott's arrival came, and waking up with the thought that I would see my husband was exhilarating. I sprang out of bed, made a cuppa and worked out how to look my best for him, which wasn't always easy. He would arrive at around lunchtime, on the mid-morning flight from LA. It was a mammoth journey and I knew he would be shattered.

I was going to surprise him with a room at the Marriott. Lord knows we had clocked up plenty of reward points, given it was our home for the first two and a half months. I jumped onto the light rail to the airport, excited like a five-year-old on Christmas morning.

It was hot, so I'd dressed a bit more casually than the last time I went to greet him, in white jeans and a hot-pink T-shirt. My hair had grown since I'd seen him last and I was hoping he'd like my latest style. I stood in my usual spot and waited, then I saw him. He walked towards me, smiled, dropped his bag and put his big muscular arms around me. I cuddled into his chest, smelled him and it felt like home.

We sat in a restaurant talking about the girls, mainly Morgan's dance teaching and Remy's schooling. I had been in touch with Remy's teachers and as tough as things had been, she was on track to graduate. I was so proud of her. My condition was not going to stop that happening. No way, I wouldn't let it.

Then we went back to the hotel room and we cuddled and loved each other, just like I'd imagined.

Scott knew I was nervous about my scans as always, so he distracted me with ideas about which little adventure we could go on once we got the results. We decided we would take a trip to Crater Lake – we had heard quite a bit about it and it sounded amazing.

Scott hadn't met Mo and Ralph yet and I couldn't wait to introduce them. Ralph had offered us his spare car to use, so Scott was also pumped about that.

Scan day arrived along with all the awful feelings, and so did a visit from the mean monster. *You do know some people regress after a few months*, he said. *You probably should go home to your family. You're just buying more time and sending them broke in the process.* His words were gut-wrenching. I blurted that out to Scott and he said, 'Don't be silly, you're going to be fine.' He said it with such conviction that I believed him. Thank god I had him with me.

I drank my radioactive concoction, had the scans and left the building. From that moment my stomach would churn more than usual. The wait between scans and results is the worst; if you've been there you'll know what I mean. The only word I can use to describe that passage of time is cruel. Torture, actually. We went downtown and wandered the streets where we noticed a small market. There was an artist sketching portraits and she called us over. On a whim we sat down and let her do her thing. When she handed us the finished product, we were astonished. It was an amazing likeness – but what struck me the most was, while my husband looked directly at the artist, my eyes appeared glazed and unfocussed, as if staring off into an uncertain future.

Scott had some lunch but I couldn't eat. We sat together in silence until the ringtone of our local phone jolted us. It was Doctor Urba, the results were in.

Chapter Thirty-three

Scott took the call. I was watching him, my stomach doing backflips. He nodded for a while, then looked at me and gave me a thumbs-up. Relief flooded my body. I didn't know what the thumbs-up meant because Scott went on to ask him if there was any progress about me getting treatment at home in Australia, and I could tell there was no positive news on that front. He didn't even put me on the phone. He finished the call and I waited with bated breath to hear the outcome.

Once again, there was shrinkage to *all* of the tumours. Not a huge amount, but shrinkage nevertheless. My relief changed to a little bit of disappointment that they hadn't all disappeared. It's not a great feeling, having tumours in your body. If you allow yourself, you can feel very much like a walking time bomb. Scott also arranged to see Doctor Urba the following week so we could delve further into the findings and do our fundraising shoot.

We wanted to get out of the city and do our road trip down to Crater Lake. Everyone in Portland raves about it as one of the top five places to visit in Oregon. Mo and Ralph picked us up that day and I proudly introduced them to my husband. We stayed the night at their place in Washington and we all got on like a house on fire. Ralph then kindly lent us his SUV so we could go exploring.

The trip down to Crater Lake was picturesque, as is mostly the case when travelling in Oregon. We had booked in to a quirky little vacation park we had found online which consisted of four separate cottages, each one with a different theme. We chose the Wild West cottage which had a log fire and pool table with funky little Western pieces scattered around the place; the main feature was a Cherokee man with a very serious look on his face. Not a real person, a statue, thankfully.

We arrived at reception to check in and on the counter was a picture of a woman with two dates underneath the photo. The day she was born and the day she died. She was the partner of the owner and she had died from cancer six months earlier. It hit me hard and I knew Scott would know what I was thinking. It seemed that every time I was feeling up I would be confronted with something that would knock me back down. I would just go quiet when I was face to face with symbols of my own mortality and he would quickly try to distract me. But that afternoon, just as I was plummeting into a depressive state, the nice monster showed up. He said, *Julie, you are going to make this, just believe me, you will see your grandchildren.* I snapped back into the present and started smiling like a Cheshire cat. I could see Scott was a little perplexed at my change in demeanour but he didn't ask why, he just went with it.

It was too late to start exploring that day, so we lit a fire outside, ate some food and sang our way through one of our favourite playlists, talking about the music and artists and our favourite songs from the past. I remember that night with total clarity. It was special. I felt connected to the moon, the stars, the universe and to my husband like never before.

The night air was getting chilly, so we went inside and put some logs on the fire. I suggested we play strip pool – I had secretly purchased a hot-pink bra and undie ensemble on special at Victoria's Secret in anticipation, and it was well hidden under my track pants and woolly jumper. Would you believe it, I played like a champion when all I wanted to do was miss shots and get my gear off! My good luck finally ran out and my husband's eyes nearly popped out of his head when he saw what was underneath my daggy exterior. I had made a decision that I was going to enjoy my life; I would be a happy, fun, sexy woman until the end, whenever that may be.

We had so much fun that night. Scott even tried – unsuccessfully – to teach me how to play chess! The next morning we headed off to the lake. What a vista! We drove up to the highest point and looked down at this magnificent waterway created after a volcano erupted over 7000 years ago. It is a sea in the middle of nowhere with no outlets or passages to waterways or the ocean. Spectacular! Then we hired a kayak and paddled down the rapids nearby. Do yourself a favour, put Oregon on your must-see list. It was inadvertently put on mine and for that I will always be grateful.

———

Making the video for the Cancer Center was harder than I'd anticipated, mainly because we had to tell my story from the beginning. Reliving my feelings when I was given my prognosis was quite traumatic and exacerbated my sense of isolation from my daughters. I was there in Portland because of my love for and promise to my girls, but they were a long way away fending for themselves. They had people around them, but it was *me* they wanted, their mother, and I couldn't be there. They were scared. It broke my heart. I decided in that moment I would sneak home again with Scott – he wasn't happy, but that was too bad. I had to see them, hug them and reassure them. It wasn't in the budget but fuck the budget, I was going home to my kids and my dog.

We couldn't leave before my treatment and appointment with Doctor Urba. He loved seeing Scott and vice versa, and I just happily sat there while they talked about boy things. He explained that my results were good but still not great and it was important to keep going with the treatment. Scott would always end our meetings with the same questions: 'How can I get my wife back home?' and 'How can we get access to this drug in Australia?' Doctor Urba said he talked to the drug company on a weekly basis and as yet they were not prepared to break the protocol of the two-year trial. But he would keep trying. We knew he would, we trusted him with my life, literally. The most frustrating thing of all was that we had learned that clinical trials had begun with this drug for advanced melanoma in Australia but if I broke the protocol in America I would not be eligible to join a trial at home.

After my treatment we secretly headed home to our girls, the three of them, Morgan, Remy and Roxy. And if I wasn't ecstatic enough, we were upgraded to business class. Very nice indeed. We had clocked up a few points by then. I figured if anyone deserved it, we did.

We knew better than to expect a cast of thousands and a marching band at the airport, we were just happy to be back home with our girls. Roxy went berserk for at least ten minutes when I arrived – she fell down, puffing and panting. The girls came home and greeted me with 'Mummmmy!' and 'Mumma!' and great big hugs. I hung on tightly, trying to comprehend and reconcile the crazy situation I had put my family in.

The time always went fast when I was home, and soon it was time to go back and sit in my chair. I knew Scott wasn't coming with me; he couldn't for a lot of reasons. Facing the realisation that I was going back alone was soul destroying. Morgan's 21st birthday was in three weeks' time. I wouldn't be there to see my beautiful daughter turn 21, the milestone we all think about from the time our kids are born. The thought of missing it was sickening. We hadn't even spoken about my return flight. I knew it was booked, I knew Scott would have done it and I knew when I had to be back.

It was the night before I had to leave and I was up in my room, packing. Morgan came to the door. She looked at me and said, 'Don't go back, Mumma, I want you here, I can't do this without you anymore.' She was howling. I wanted to howl with her but I had to be strong.

'I have to go, Morgs, but Dad will be here.'

'But you want Dad with you, Mum, I know you do.'

'I'll be fine, darling, and we can have your 21st party next time I'm home.'

'I don't want to have my party without you,' she said.

'I'll be back, I promise.' I started to beat myself up for what I had put my children through. I should have waited and somehow tried to come home for her birthday. But her birthday was on a treatment day; it was impossible.

The morning came and I wanted to get up and run. Run away so no one could find me. I didn't want to leave my family, my husband, my girls, my dog, my dad, my sisters, my brother, my friends. Why did I have to? It wasn't fair! The sensible monster decided to make an appearance. *Hey, shouldn't you be grateful you are alive and that the treatment is working? Even if it is slowly. It could be a lot worse.* He was right but I couldn't help wallowing in self-pity. Nothing was going to lift me out of my despair that day. I went out the back with my dog and ran and sang my song, choking back the tears as I tried to regather. But I couldn't keep running, I had to go back home, and go back to America and do what I had promised to do.

I said goodbye to my girls, trying not to look as angry on the outside as I felt on the inside. Scott put my bags in the car and we drove to the airport in silence. I checked in and we sat down at a table. He had a coffee and I had a brandy. I had to try something to stop my uncontrollable crying, but it didn't work. My tears were dropping onto the table. I didn't care. Everyone was looking at me and I didn't care about that either. Then Scott suddenly realised he had booked me on the 4pm flight from LA to Portland instead of the 10am and he was distraught. That would mean I had a whole day at LA airport. He was running around trying to change my flight while I sat at the table crying. He couldn't change it.

My flight was called and I had to go. I hugged him but I couldn't look at him. I was a monumental wreck. I turned, walked through the door and didn't look back. I couldn't; I wouldn't have kept going if I did. I was still crying and I still didn't care. I howled my way through security and onto the plane. Scott called from the carpark. He didn't think I'd get on the plane. I didn't sleep a wink from Sydney to LA, then spent eight excruciating hours at LA airport trying to keep my eyes open before boarding the next flight. I landed in Portland and by that stage I was in zombie mode.

Standing at the baggage carousel, I felt a tap on my shoulder. Scott had called Monique and asked her to pick me up. That was a lovely surprise, but I still felt numb. I stayed with her and Ralph that night. She dropped me home in the morning and I walked over to the hospital, sat in my chair and got my infusion of the drug that was keeping me alive. Mo and Ralph had offered a room at their place permanently, but I needed to be close to the hospital, and they lived an hour away and both had to work. Although it was a beautiful country environment, I would have been even more isolated.

My dad had offered to come back to America with me and I knew he meant it, but he was getting older and it was such a long trip. If something went wrong, the medical system was brutal in terms of cost. He didn't need that worry. But a few days after I arrived back he called me and convinced me to take him up on his offer.

My generous and beautiful brother, Mark, organised his flights and flew him over to be with me. He would arrive the following week. In all this darkness, I thought to myself, *If my life ends tomorrow I have been blessed to be a part of the best family in the world.*

Ralph and I went to pick up Dad from the airport and to my relief he'd arrived safely and in one piece. We went to a sports bar where we chatted away happily for a couple of hours. Dad and Ralph clicked straight away, connecting with their love of sports and American politics. We visited Ralph's restaurant and played mini putt-putt. Mo took us to the markets and out for dinner.

I would go to yoga in the afternoons and then meet Dad at the local pub for a pre-dinner drink. We would talk about his childhood and his schooldays and his work life. I learned more about my father in those two weeks than in the previous 50 years of my life. I will treasure that time forever and am so grateful I had him all to myself. He would come to treatments with me and flirt with the nurses, which was a tad embarrassing, but I think they took it in the spirit in which it was intended. Dad put up with a lot from me in those two weeks. I was frustrated and emotional about being away from the girls, and I was missing Scott like crazy. Dad, of all humans, would understand how much I was aching for my husband. He still ached for my mum and she had been gone for eleven and a half years at that time.

Soon I sadly said goodbye to my dad. He had medical appointments back home.

The morning after he left I woke up and there was blood everywhere, coming from inside me. I freaked out. *What's happening to me?* My first thought was the tumours. *Something's happened, something's gone wrong in there and I'm going to bleed to death. The tumours have become too big and burst inside me.* I was hysterical. Then I went to the bathroom and realised what had happened. It was my period. I had come out of menopause. Then it dawned on me that when I'd stopped the chemo seven months earlier, my body had decided to start producing eggs again. I didn't know it was possible to come out of menopause, especially at 51 years of age. *Gee, I'm one lucky gal,* I said to myself sarcastically, but felt comfort in how amazing my body was to rejuvenate itself like that. I thanked it for being so clever.

The day was coming and I was dreading it – 3 September 2013 in the US, which meant it was soon to be 4 September in Australia, Morgan's 21st birthday. I tried to occupy my day with as much as I could by running and writing in my journal. I pondered over what sort of mother I had been. I knew I wasn't expecting any 'mother of the year' awards any time soon. I figured I was about a seven and a half out of ten and wondered what score my girls would give me. Maybe it was best I didn't ask.

I had arranged to Skype at 4pm, which would be nine in the morning on Morgan's birthday. I sat at my computer in my humble accommodation and called her number. I was already gulping down the lumps in my throat. There was that funny, unique Skype noise and then there they were, all of them and more. They were on the deck of our home with balloons and streamers and a fun party atmosphere that Scott had secretly prepared the night before, after the girls went to bed.

I was devastated I wasn't there, but thankful that Morgan looked happy. She deserved it. She had been through so much. I managed to keep it together and she showed me all her presents and Remy joked about 'where was her present' because when the girls were little I would always give the other one a small gift to ease the blow of not being the birthday girl. Morgan angled the camera down to Roxy, who started whimpering and trying to paw at the screen. I think there was a little champagne involved as they all seemed silly and giggly. Then I glanced over to the side of the screen where my husband was cooking their breakfast on the barbecue. I was watching him flipping the eggs and turning the bacon and when he turned around and saw me on the screen, his face changed and he gave me the most loving look I had ever seen and he simply said, 'There she is' and in that moment I felt like the luckiest person in the world.

Morgan gave me the date for her party. 'I'll be there,' I said. I told her I loved her and wished her the best birthday ever. I had to go. I was just about to lose it.

While emotionally shattered, I managed to find the resolve and determination to get through the following few weeks without too much distress for myself and others. But when scan time was approaching I became a nervous wreck. Scott came back over. I tried to be brave and pretend I would be okay, but he knew I was struggling. If I had a bad result and I was on my own, it would be unbearable. I am the ultimate optimist, but also a realist. This was around the six-month mark, when for some patients things can take a turn for the worse.

Yet again the scans were good, the tumours were still slowly but surely shrinking away. Even Doctor Urba was amazed, as most people had plateaued out and didn't respond any further after six months. We met with him that day and again we begged him to find a way to get me home to my family.

I was reaching the end of my tether. Scott asked him what he would do if it were his wife and he was in the same position as us. 'Well,' he said in his beautiful accent, 'if it were my wife I would want her to stay and continue with the treatment. But I know you have children at home in Australia and there's a chance this treatment could work for twelve months or two years, even further, and there's also a chance that the drug could stop working and things could get worse and Julie could die, and I get that you would not want to spend the last years of your life away from your family.' Then there was silence.

To break the ice I said, 'You were going really well there, Doctor Urba, until you said that bit about dying.' He thought I was funny but I think we all knew I was using the humour to mask the inner turmoil the 'd' word had stirred up inside me.

Then, somehow my husband clandestinely found the name of a person who worked for the drug company that made the drug I had been on, Bristol-Myers Squibb. He has never told me how and I have never asked, because I think he might have gone snooping around in Doctor Urba's office when he pulled the curtains to examine me. He found the name of a woman in the clinical trials area, guessed her email address and sent her a deeply heartfelt letter begging her to let us get back home to our family in Australia. The email didn't bounce back so he was hopeful, but nervous that he was crossing the line. It was more likely, he thought, that he would be ignored. He just had to wait.

I didn't know how to feel after our conversation with Doctor Urba, but one thing I did know was we had been given a wonderful gift from my angel Shari Scales and the team at the Providence Foundation for helping them out with the fundraising video and also as a little surprise for Scott's birthday. They shouted us three nights at the most divine five-star resort, the Allison Inn & Spa in the Willamette Valley, in Oregon wine country. I was really looking forward to that time in luxury with my husband, and the doctor's frankness had momentarily taken off the shine. Scott did ask the question, though. We wanted an honest answer and we certainly got one. I thought of nothing else all the way there. But as soon as we checked in

I made a decision to stay steadfastly in the moment and make the most of our time there. We visited wineries (not that I could indulge), went for walks, had massages and listened to music. Good times! I was enjoying my life. I had promised myself I would, and I like to keep my promises.

A couple of days later I received an email from one of Remy's teachers to say she had completed all of the necessary Year 12 modules, so she would graduate at the end of September. There would be a ceremony at the school followed by a lunch, and her school formal would be that same night. I had already missed one of her formals, which had crushed me to numbness, and I sure as hell was not going to miss another one. Scott just went quiet when I announced I would be going back home for that event and nothing was going to stop me. I was done missing out on my children's milestones and the fact that my baby had managed to graduate under those circumstances was close to a miracle. I was so proud of her. She could have just bailed out, but she knew how important it was for all of us as a family. I wanted so badly for her to learn this invaluable life lesson – triumph over adversity is possible and we become stronger and more grateful human beings despite the pain and the fear we have endured.

Along with heartache, this journey had cost us financially, but it was difficult to think about that when my life was in the balance. I know I am stating the bleeding obvious that airfares are not cheap and at some stage soon that luxury had to come to an end. But not now, I thought, I just have to get back for her graduation and Morgan's 21st birthday party. I called Remy and excitedly told her I was coming. She was over the moon.

I asked her to put Morgan on the phone and told her I would be back for her party. Thank god the timing worked out and yet again I would be able to sneak home to my girls.

Scott stayed back at the apartment to pack while I went across the road to have my infusion. All I wanted to do was express my excitement about going home and the important events I would experience while I was there, but I had to zipper up. As I've said, the nurses loved hearing about our upcoming adventures but I couldn't tell them about this one. I was practically out of my seat before the needle was out of my chest. I had a plane to catch. Well, two, actually.

The graduation was an emotional and surreal experience. When they called her name, Remy Randall, the tears streamed down my face. I had to keep my sunnies on. *You amazing little girl,* I thought, *how on earth did you manage it?* This was another bittersweet day for me. I felt a lot of eyes staring at me – most people knew what was going on, of course, but one woman I didn't know very well made a beeline for me and asked me this question: 'How is your health?' I was stunned. I had been standing there with my family with a grin from ear to ear once I got over the tears and she felt it necessary to intrude on that moment and ask me such an invasive, personal question. Apparently because you have had an illness, although I don't like to use that term, you are obliged to tell anyone and everyone your business.

Somehow I think she knew I didn't appreciate her question when I responded with, 'Good, how's yours?'

It just floors me that you can be at a celebration, laughing and enjoying yourself, and someone would think you'd be happy to be interrupted, answer very personal questions and be taken back to a place in your mind where you don't want to go. If I wanted to talk about my health with anyone, I would approach the person and politely ask, 'Do you mind if we talk about my health?' I can assure you that will never happen. A good, old-fashioned 'How are you?' is perfect. But then again, as I have said, that's just me.

Remy looked stunning in her hot-pink formal dress that night. We went to pre-dinner drinks with her and her friends, then left her to enjoy her night. She delivered the news the next morning that she had become a little excited, had too much to drink on the way to the function and been given a 'chill-out card', which meant she had to sit outside until she sobered up. I laughed at the thought of her sitting there with that cheeky little grin on her face. Probably not what a normal, responsible mother would do, but there was nothing normal about our lives at the time.

Morgan's 21st party was fabulous. Scott and I couldn't bring ourselves to do a serious speech, as we would have been extremely lucky to get the first sentence out, so he said some fun words and I wrote and performed a rap song. I recruited some of her friends to do the back-up vocals. I think it went over pretty well.

We danced and laughed and sang and I was the happiest woman on the planet.

The following Monday morning, as I lay in bed watching Scott get ready for work, I was thanking the universe for my adorable family and the special times we had just had when he made a statement that completely ruined my heavenly thoughts.

'I'm booking your flight back to Portland today. You will have to leave on Wednesday, darl.'

'I'm not going back,' I announced. 'I just can't go back. I want to be at home.' It had now become clear that we couldn't afford for Scott to fly back and forth anymore, nor would I be able to come back home for visits. So how could I say goodbye to my girls this time, knowing we couldn't afford any more airfares? I had been crying with my sister Michelle the day before, dangling our legs into the lake near our home, and like everyone else she felt helpless. She knew I had exhausted all avenues and she knew I would miss seeing my baby girl turn eighteen. I had been living in Portland for seven months and would have to stay for another seventeen if the treatment kept working.

'You're going back,' he said. 'I'm booking your flight.'

'I'm not fucking going back!' I shouted and threw a pillow at him across the room.

'Darl, you have to go back.' I followed him downstairs and kept up with my protest, with four-letter words coming thick and fast. He walked out the door and I slammed it behind him. Thank god the girls weren't there and Roxy had already hidden behind the sofa. I slid down the back of the door and sat there crying and banging the palms of my hands into my forehead. I had been living in America for so many months and even after all that time I was still in disbelief at what our world had become. I knew I was behaving irrationally. Like a spoilt brat, actually. I knew I had to go back, I had promised my children I'd do whatever it took.

I stayed there for about fifteen minutes before I pushed myself up off the wooden floorboards, walked over to the kettle and flicked the switch. I was trying to calm myself down when something compelled me to turn on my computer and look at my emails. I noticed an email from the Mater Hospital in Sydney, so I clicked on it, put on my glasses and began to read.

> Dear Julie,
>
> Your next infusion of Nivolumab will be administered at the Patricia Ritchie Centre at the Mater Hospital in Crows Nest, Sydney, Australia. Please call to set up an appointment.

I was shaking. I read it again and again and again.

I ran up the stairs and, don't ask me why, dived onto the bed and started punching the pillows – well, one was still on the floor, the one I'd thrown at Scott's head. I ran back down the stairs, lay on the floor, cuddled the dog and started laughing, crying and screaming at the same time. I was running around in circles mimicking Roxy's happy dance. Then I jumped up, ran back to my computer and read the email again. I walked onto our deck and looked out at the park. I pinched myself as hard as I could to make sure I was awake and not dreaming.

I would be staying home with my precious family for good. I called Scott and tried to sound calm. 'Have you booked those flights yet?'

'No,' he said sombrely, 'I was just about to.'

I said, 'Well don't, because you'll be wasting our money. I have just sent you an email. Open it up.'

There was silence and then, 'WOW! Is this for real?' I heard him choking up. He couldn't speak; his relief was palpable. And that theme continued as I made call after call to my girls, who both cried with happiness, and then my family and my friends. I couldn't wait to tell my mum. It turns out Scott's email to the drug company Bristol-Myers Squibb got through, and while I'm pretty sure it's not how things are supposed to work, it must have struck a chord with someone, who campaigned to get us home. I love those people. You see, I wasn't just Patient 71 anymore, I wasn't just a number, I was a real person with children and loved ones and a dog and a home and a life back in Australia. Their email was telling me I could go home to Australia! Ironically, unbeknown to them, I was already in Australia, and now I was here to stay. I became the first person in this country to receive the drug now known as Nivolumab outside a clinical trial. They had granted me compassionate use of this life-saving drug. It had really happened. I'd found my way back home.

Epilogue

Today I am still living on the Northern Beaches with my precious little family. If I could take away the pain and trauma this mammoth journey inflicted on them, I would. But I would do it all again in a heartbeat to stay with my daughters. I have my baby girls and they have their mum. They can now go back to worrying about what to wear out on the weekends. That makes me the happiest mother in the world. My husband has gone back to heavily guarding his sock drawer – *that* makes me smile. Sadly we lost our beloved Roxy in 2015. I miss her every day. The rest of my family are all doing well. We still get together just like before and usually laugh until we cry.

I still have a monthly infusion of Nivolumab at the Mater Hospital and have become great friends with all the nurses. I mix up my appointment times and arrive late; I'm probably their naughtiest patient, surprise surprise! But they love me just the same. I have made peace with the mean monster, but he still pops in from time to time.

Nivolumab (also called Opdivo), along with many other immunotherapy drugs, is now filtering into the medical arena, which makes my heart sing as it is creating hope for cancer patients where there was little or none before. I am convinced this therapy will be the way of the future and I am proud to be part of the science behind it.

Scott and I returned to Portland in May 2015 to speak at a fundraiser for the hospital. We were honoured to have the opportunity to help raise money for research, which in turn will equate to saving more lives. We are going back there again this year to speak at the 'Creating Hope' fundraising dinner, which is really exciting.

We keep in touch with Mo and Ralph, now our lifelong friends, and we will stay in their country home as we did last time. I keep in contact with Doctor Urba and all of my friends from Providence.

Scott and I also spoke at a conference for Bristol-Myers Squibb in Miami in 2015 to share our story with their sales team. A life and a family saved because of the drugs they had developed and their relentless, ongoing research. The sales team are the front line for the company, and they were all touched and motivated by our story.

I visit the professor, who is now my friend, every three months and during my last visit I asked her what she thought my future looked like. This is what she said: 'Julie, I now say that we can cure about a third of my patients and it is highly likely that you are one of them.'

Through teary eyes I responded with, 'I know I'm one of them.' And in that moment a wave of emotion washed over me from head to toe as I came to the realisation that I had kept the promise I had made to my daughters on that fateful night.

On 21 June 2017 it will be five years since I suddenly collapsed that afternoon in the office. I have been taken from the depths of despair to a new and exciting world where I feel I am meant to be. I love helping and inspiring people *and* I discovered I love to write. One by one I am ticking off all the things I have promised myself I would do. Scott and I have formed a band with a few friends; we're called The Lucky Stones. I don't think you'll see us on iTunes any time soon, but we're sure having a lot of fun *and* we celebrated our twenty-fifth wedding anniversary in November 2016. My future is now as bright and as colourful as a rainbow – for that I am grateful every single day. I know many people don't make it through this devastatingly brutal condition. For their families, my heart bleeds because I have been in their shoes.

Somebody recently asked me what I had learned from my ordeal and I answered with the following:

Life is only too short if you sell yourself short; *you* are capable of far more than you ever dreamed possible.

Don't wait until you're told you're dying to truly start living.

If you have that nagging feeling that there is something more for you to do in life – act on it.

It is imperative that you take control of your own destiny in sickness and in health. There is a big wide world out there and you have it at your fingertips, literally.

Use sunscreen daily and take care of your skin, it's the largest organ you have.

The voices of fear are trying to keep you safe and protect you from disappointment, but you will only be disappointed if you believe what they are telling you.

Put fun and laughter first, not last.

Look into your children's eyes and listen when they talk to you.

Bring more love and music into your life.

These things I know for sure.

Do I sweat the small stuff now, you ask? Yes I do, because I'm human.

Do I stress about the big stuff now? No I don't, I just believe.

———

If you are wondering how I am right now, well, I have a little song that sums it up perfectly. A song that a very nice monster taught me when my future looked bleak. It goes something like this:

I am happy and healthy,
All my organs have healed,
My body and its organs are healed,
I have faith in life.

Acknowledgements

There were so many wonderful people by my side on this journey of survival who I wanted to thank personally in this book so I sat down and wrote a list of names. It turned out to be six pages long and I would wake up in the middle of the night thinking of more people. The list seemed endless and then I realised it was. If I left anyone off that list I would be mortified. So I decided it was best not to go there. Not to mention I wasn't allocated enough pages!

So I want to say to everyone who helped us in any way, big or small, we appreciate your love, kindness and generosity more than you will ever know.

To our friends and family in Australia we thank you all from the bottom of our hearts.

To my Providence family headed up by the remarkable Doctor Walter Urba, it is hard to find words to express our love and gratitude. Thank you for allowing me to stay in the world so I can be the mother, wife, daughter, sister and friend that I long to be for many years to come.

To all of the 'Squibbys' at BMS, thank you for allowing me to come home to Australia and be with my people.

To Mo and Ralph, you took me into your hearts at a time when loneliness consumed me. Thank you isn't enough.

To Cindy and Steve Harder, thank you for everything.

To Marianne Dodds, thank you for being at the other end of the phone whenever we needed you, even in Portland.

To Stephanie Moody, thank you for introducing me to yoga. It allowed me to experience pockets of peace and quiet from the loud noises inside my head.

To Georgina and Anna from the Melanoma Institute of Australia, thank you for looking after me and taking a genuine interest in my family's wellbeing.

To my new friends at the Patricia Ritchie Centre, thanks for making my ongoing treatment more like 'lunch with the girls'.

Thank you Andrew Fraser for going above and beyond the call of duty and looking after my publishing deal.

To Marg, thanks so much for your love and support as always.

To the sisterhood, the dance mums, and all of my close friends – you know who you are. I am forever grateful to have you in my life.

To my dad, you are an amazing human being. One of the best, actually. Thank you for your love and generosity. I loved having you with me in Portland.

To my mum in heaven, thanks for listening and bringing me up to be a tough cookie.

To my brother and sisters and their families, thank you for your unwavering love in good times and in bad. I know I can count on you for anything. Especially a drink and a laugh.

To my two rays of sunshine, Morgan and Remy, my babies, my soldiers. I'm sorry you had to grow up so fast. I am so proud of the people you are. I thank you from the depths of my heart for being strong and coming out the other side as better human beings.

Finally to my husband, Scott. You went out on a limb for me, making unqualified comments such as 'You'll be right, Darl,' and 'You're not going anywhere, Darl,' and 'Never in doubt, Darl.' You believed in me when others thought we were fighting a losing battle. I hung on to your words. You loved me back to life. I love you more than I thought anyone could love another.

Made in the USA
Middletown, DE
12 September 2021